GENTLE GIANTS
AN EMOTIONAL FACE TO FACE WITH DOLPHINS AND WHALES

WHITE STAR PUBLISHERS

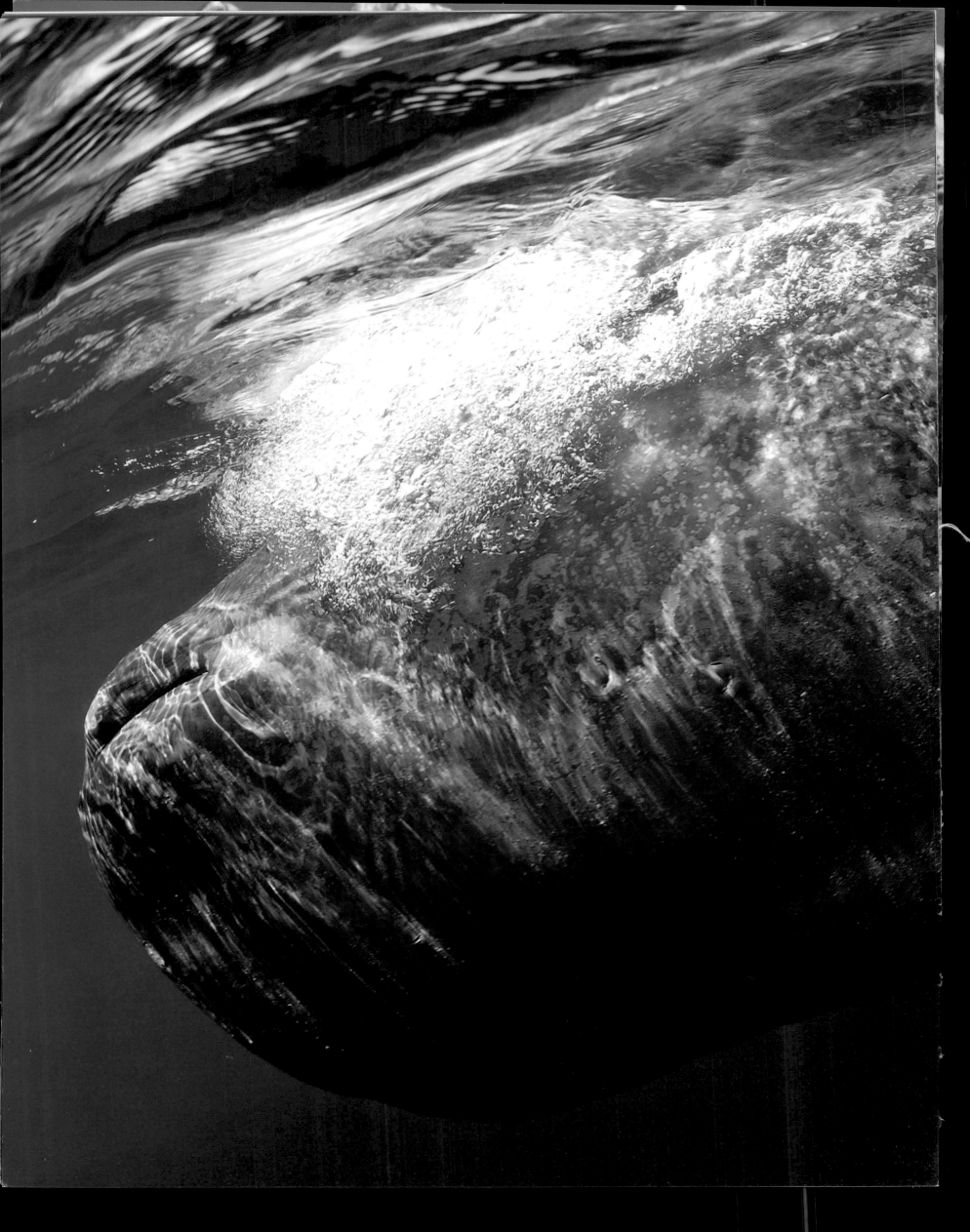

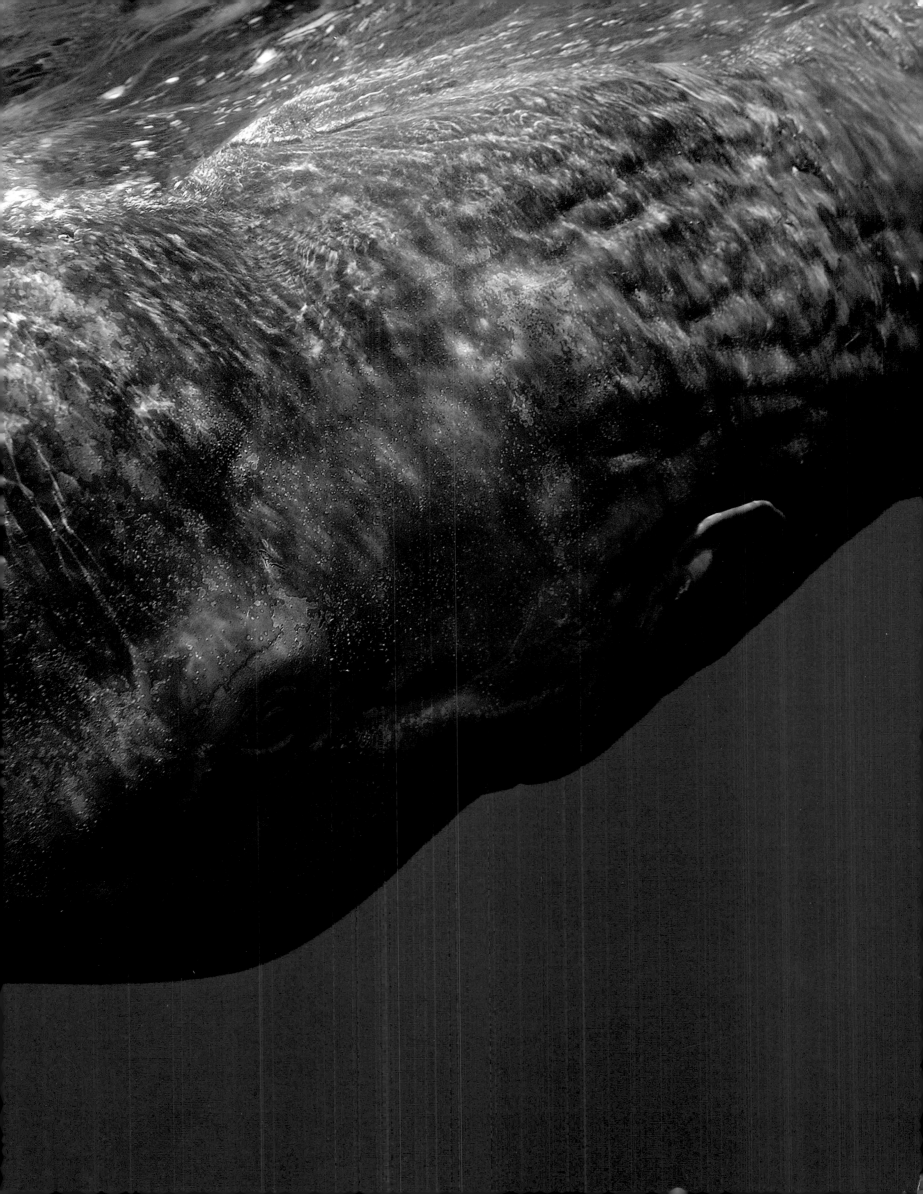

CETACEANS DEFINED
A LOOK INTO THE DIVERSE WORLD OF WHALES, DOLPHINS AND PORPOISES

CETACEANS DEFINED

A LOOK INTO THE DIVERSE WORLD OF WHALES, DOLPHINS AND PORPOISES

Whales, dolphins and porpoises are collectively known as cetaceans, derived from the Latin word Cetus, meaning "whale." They are some of the most distinctive and specialized mammals on Earth.

Currently 87 species of cetaceans are recognized, but the number keeps changing, and scientists always have to reclassify some species and add more as they learn about the animals' behaviours, genetic identities and evolutionary histories. Several species such as killer whales are relatively easy to recognize. Others differ from one another only in subtle ways and are hard to identify at sea. Some species are so rare or elusive that they are seldom sighted and very little is known about them. Several beaked whales, for example, are known only from stranded specimens and have never been seen alive. It was not until 2002 that a new species of beaked whale, Perrin's beaked whale (*Mesoplodon perrini*), was formally recognized, and the latest genetic research is revealing that some animals previously thought to be single species should actually be split. It is not uncommon for one species to have two or more common names in English, and to be known as well by many other names in different parts of the world. The fin whale, for example, is also called the finner, the finback, or the razorback in English and has special local names in Japan, Norway, Greenland, Russia, France, and Spain. To overcome this difficulty, scientists have devised an international and universally recognized system of classification. Carl Linnaeus was the first to create a system for naming, ranking, and classifying organisms. According to this system, cetaceans are given a scientific Latin name with two words, the genus first, and then the species name. For example the scientific name for the fin whale is *Balaenoptera physalus*.

Naming a species is one thing, but being able to identify a whale at sea is not always straightforward. Some species are more cooperative than others and readily give some clues as to who they are. The size and shape of the dorsal fin can help in recognizing a whale. In the 1970s, Canadian researcher Michael Bigg developed a technique that revolutionized the study of killer whales. By photographing the killer whales' dorsal fin and grey saddle patch at the base of the fin, he found that individual whales had unique markings and could be identified and studied. The result was the production of the most detailed catalogue of the killer whales of British Columbia and Washington, describing family groups and genealogical relationships. Researchers also use photographs of the tail flukes of humpback whales to identify each individual. But for some species, it is not so easy. For example, even the most expert whale watchers have a hard time telling pygmy right whales apart from minke whales when they are seen at the water's surface, because of their small size, dark color, and curved dorsal fin. And it was only in 2003 that Omura's whale was confirmed as a species of its own, having a separate and ancient lineage. It was previously grouped with another species, the Bryde's whale.

Cetaceans are divided into two main groups, the toothed whales (*Odontoceti*) and the baleen whales (*Mysticeti*). Dolphins and porpoises are examples of odontocetes, as are belugas, narwhals, sperm whales, and beaked whales. They all have teeth and use echolocation to navigate. Mysticetes, or baleen whales, do not have teeth. Instead, they have plates called baleen that they use to trap food Blue, right, humpback, minke, grey, and fin whales are well-known examples of baleen whales. Another difference between the mysticetes and the odontocetes is that the baleen whales have two blowholes, and the toothed whales only have one.

There are currently 14 recognized species of baleen whales, classified into four families. There is an ongoing debate about the precise number of species, and genetic analyses will undoubtedly continue to influence revisions of mysticete taxonomy. Baleen whales are generally large animals. The smallest, the pygmy right whale, grows to about 20 feet (6 m) while the blue whale reaches more than 100 feet (30 m) and can weigh more than 100 tons. Large size may be an adaptation related to food storage or heat conservation in cold water, but the evolution of this characteristic is not well understood.

With the exception of the pygmy right whale, all of the baleen whales were subject to heavy exploitation by the whaling industry, which severely depleted many populations. While some species appear to be recovering well, some remain highly vulnerable to extinction.

The largest family of baleen whales is the family Balaenopteridae, also known as the rorquals. This family includes the humpback whale (*Megaptera novaeangliae*), the minke whale (*Balaenoptera acutorostrata*), the Antarctic minke whale (*Balaenoptera bonaerensis*), Bryde's whale (*Balaenoptera edeni*), the Sei whale (*Balaenoptera borealis*), the fin whale (*Balaenoptera physalus*), the blue whale (*Balaenoptera musculus*), and Omura's whale (*Balaenoptera omurai*).

Rorquals are slender and streamlined in shape. They have a dorsal fin, short baleen plates, and heads that are flat on top rather than arched or curved like those of other baleen whales. Most have narrow, elongated flippers. They have a large number of throat pleats to allow the mouth to expand immensely when feeding. The largest of the rorquals, the blue whale, weighs 15 times as much as the smallest, the minke whale. The fin whale is the second largest animal on Earth after the blue whale, and is also one of the fastest swimmers, capable of bursts of speed of up to 23 mph (37 kph). Bryde's whales are the least known of this group, and are unusual compared to their relatives because they do not seem to migrate long distances between feeding and breeding grounds every year.

Humpbacks are a whale watcher's favourite. They are one of the most energetic and acrobatic whales, often displaying full body breaches, tail- and flipper-slaps, and surface lunges. They grow up to 50 feet (15 m), and can weigh up to 40 tons. Their extraordinary pectoral fins, which are about one-third as long as the body, are one of the most remarkable features of humpbacks. They are slower swimmer than the other rorquals, and have captured the imagination of humans for their extraordinary ability to sing. Humpback whales have a number of rounded protuberances, called tubercles, on their heads and lower jaws. The various knobs, folds, bumps, and creases of a humpback's body are host to a variety of parasites, particularly barnacles. These do not actually feed off the whale, but rather use the whale as a ship, which gives them the opportunity to feed on microscopic marine organisms on their free ride across the oceans.

18-19 The humpback whale is one of the most exciting whales to watch. It is very active at the surface, engaging in a variety of behaviors. The most spectacular humpback display is the breach. Some humpbacks have been observed breaching more than 80 times in a row.

The family Balaenidae includes four species of right whales, the bowhead whale, also known as the Greenland right whale (*Balaena mysticetus*), the North Atlantic right whale (*Eubalaena glacialis*), the North Pacific right whale (*Eubalaena japonica*), and the Southern right whale (*Eubalaena australis*). The term "right whale" was given by whalers who considered them as the "right" whales to kill. They were fat with oil and had long, valuable baleen. They were also slow swimmers, floated when harpooned to death, and were easy to find because they bred in coastal waters. They were among the first species to be heavily exploited by whalers, and all of them came close to extinction.

Found only in Arctic and sub-arctic waters, the bowhead whale received its name from the high, arched upper jaw that somewhat resembles the shape of an archer's bow. With its thick blubber and its ability to create its own breathing holes by breaking through ice, the bowhead is well adapted to its freezing environment. Bowhead whales have been an important subsistence item for arctic native communities for centuries.

The southern and northern right whales look almost identical, but they are separate species. Right whales lack a dorsal fin, and they have callosities, raised roughened patches of skin, mostly around their heads, that are home for barnacles and whale lice. Southern right whales had been studied for decades, when scientists started to identify individuals by the shape and pattern of the callosities on their heads in Peninsula Valdés, Argentina. They are demonstrative and inquisitive whales, and are often seen breaching, spyhopping (when a whale pokes its head above the surface of the wa-

ter), and lobtailing (when a whale slaps its flukes against the surface of the water). Their population is increasing, a stark contrast with the North Atlantic right whale, which faces the risk of extinction.

The North Atlantic and North Pacific right whales have never recovered from whaling, and are the most endangered whales in the world. Even though the whaling of their species has ceased, North Atlantic right whales are now threatened by collisions with boats and entanglement in fishing gear. They range in the coastal waters of eastern North America from the Canadian Maritimes to Florida, regions heavily used by the military and by fishing and shipping industries. The current population is believed to be about 300 to 350 individuals.

The family Neobalaenidae has only one species, the pygmy right whale (*Caperea marginata*), as does the family Eschrichtiidae, which has a single member, the grey whale (*Eschrichtius robustus*). The pygmy right whale is the smallest of the baleen whales, growing to scarcely 20 feet (6 m) and weighing only three to four tons. Because of its small size, it has never been commercially hunted. It is rarely seen at sea, and very little is known about this whale.

Unlike the pygmy right whale, the grey whale was heavily hunted, and was driven to extinction in the North Atlantic. The Western Pacific population of grey whales has only about 100 animals remaining, but the Eastern North Pacific population recovered exceptionally well from whaling. Once called the "devilfish" by whalers because of their violent defensive behaviours, they are now known for sometimes displaying friendly behaviour and curiosity towards boats. In the grey whale, a series of bumps replace the dorsal fin. Barnacles grow in various places on the body of the grey whale, and are usually most obvious on the head.

The magnificent sperm whale, also known as cachalot (*Physeter macrocephalus*), is the single member of the family Physeteridae. With its large head, the sperm whale acquired fame with Herman Merville's classic tale, *Moby Dick*. It is the largest toothed whale, and it grows to up to 60 feet (18 m) long in the case of males, who are much larger than the females. They have a taste for squid, which they seek at great depths. They are the deepest divers of all whales, descending to depths of more than 3300 feet (1000 m) and staying submerged for an hour or more. At sea they are easy to identify by their distinctive blowhole that slants forward at 45 degrees. Sperm whales were intensively hunted during the 19th century for body oil and the spermaceti oil contained in their heads. They can be encountered almost anywhere in the world's oceans and seas, but especially along the edges of continental and island shelves.

Baleen whales are a small group compared to the toothed whales (odontocetes), which make up the vast majority of cetaceans. There are currently 73 species of toothed whales classified into ten families, ranging from the tiny vaquita or Gulf of California porpoise, which weighs about 120 lbs (55 kg) and is about 5 feet (1.5 m) long to the sperm whale, which can reach 60 feet (18 m). In contrast to the baleen whales, odontocetes have teeth, and are active predators. They chase and catch fish, and in some cases, marine mammals such as harbour seals, sea lions, and other whales. The number and arrangement of teeth varies be-

tween species and depends on their diet. For example, the male narwhal has a single tusk while spinner dolphins have more than 170 teeth. Killer whales have long, sharp teeth to capture large prey such as marine mammals and fish. Belugas use small peg-like teeth to catch and eat small fish and crustaceans. Toothed whales move fast, and their bodies are typically smaller than baleen whales, although there are some exceptions.

The most enigmatic and the least understood of all cetaceans are the beaked whales. Found in deep ocean waters, the majority of species have been described from only a handful of specimens, found stranded on beaches. Currently 21 species of beaked whales are recognized and classified in the family Ziphiidae. Because they live in the deep and are so difficult to observe, several species have never been seen alive, and only a few have been studied in any detail. New species are regularly described and old species frequently revised. The most recent addition to the list is Perrin's beaked whale (*Mesoplodon perrini*), formally named in 2002. As their name suggests, most of the beaked whales have a pronounced beak of variable length. They also have a pair of grooves on the throat and "flipper pockets," slight depressions in the body wall into which the flippers can be tucked, perhaps to reduce drag. Their most remarkable feature is their teeth. In most species, females have no functional teeth, and males often have only one or two pairs in the lower jaw, which sometimes are exposed to the point of being tusks. Scientists have long wondered why some males have tusks and have speculated that the tusks are an ornament to help females identify males within their species, which might otherwise be difficult as the species can be quite similar to each other in shape and coloration.

Another cetacean sporting a long, spiral tusk is the narwhal (*Monodon monoceros*), a whale that lives year-round in the Arctic. With its thick layer of blubber, it is well adapted to living in extremely cold waters. Like the narwhal, the beluga (*Delphinapterus leucas*) lives in the Arctic and is a member of the family Monodontidae. The beluga is one of the most distinctive of the whales, with its white skin, lack of dorsal fin, flexible neck and expressive face. Belugas and narwhals continue to be hunted in many northern communities for their skin and in the case of the narwhal for its valuable tusk ivory. Intensive hunting in some parts of the beluga's range is the biggest known threat to the survival of this animal, although the various populations of belugas are faced with additional threats such as disturbance by vessel traffic, habitat degradation, chemical pollution, and climate change.

The family Delphinidae is the largest, with 36 species of dolphins, and its members are commonly known as "ocean dolphins." This can be confusing because some species are called "whales" and others do not dwell in the ocean but live in rivers and lakes. Members of this family vary greatly in appearance, lifestyle, habitat, and social behaviours. Some species range worldwide such as the killer whale or orca (*Orcinus orca*) while others are restricted to a particular area such as the Hector's dolphin (*Cephalorhynchus hectori*), found only in New Zealand, and currently endangered because of frequent entanglement in gillnets. The killer whale is the largest of the dolphins. Recently researchers have found strong genetic evidence supporting the theory that there are several species of killer whales throughout the world's oceans. Two types of killer whales in the Antarctic that respectively eat fish and seals are suggested as separate species, along with marine-mammal-eating "transient" killer whales in the North Pacific. One of the most studied and best-known species of ocean dolphins is the bottlenose dolphin (*Tursiops truncatus*). It had a special place in Greek and Roman mythology, and today it is the species that most often comes to mind when people think about dolphins. Scientists continue to learn about the different species of dolphins. One of the places in the world where the dolphin is appreciated more for its flesh than its friendly behaviour is in the Japanese town of Taiji, where thousands of dolphins are still slaughtered every year.

While new species are discovered, others are lost. River dolphins have colonized some of the greatest rivers in the world: the Amazon, the Ganges, the Indus, and the Yangtze. But today they are among the rarest and the most threatened cetaceans. According to Chinese legend, the Yangtze River dolphin, also known by its Chinese name baiji (*Lipotes vexillifer*), is the reincarnation of a drowned princess. This graceful freshwater dolphin has a very long, slightly upturned beak and a low triangular dorsal fin. Because it resides in muddy waters, it has little need for vision and as a result has tiny, barely functional eyes. The baiji declined due to accidental fishery by-catch and other factors associated with the industrialization of its home, the Yangtze River in China. Only 13 animals remained by the end of the 20th century, and today the Yangtze River dolphin is likely to be extinct. It was the only representative of the family Lipotidae.

The Ganges and Indus river dolphins are considered a single species and belong to the family platanisticae. Like the Yangtze River dolphin, these animals are virtually blind. Their habitat has been severely degraded, and they are endangered throughout their range. The Amazon River dolphin belongs to the family Iniidae and is often called the pink dolphin because of its pinkish color. The Amazon River dolphins have extremely flexible bodies and are able to twist and bend more than most dolphins. They can be playful and inquisitive and will sometimes approach people and boats. Found in the main rivers of the Amazon and Orinoco basins, this dolphin enters flooded jungles during the rainy season, swimming between the trees. The fourth species, the Franciscana or La Plata dolphin (*Pontoporia blainvillei*) is a river dolphin in name only. It inhabits coastal marine waters from northern Argentina to southern Brazil. It is particularly vulnerable to entanglement in gillnets.

The term "porpoise," derived from the Latin *porcus* for "pig" and *piscus* for "fish", has often been used colloquially to refer to various smaller-size cetaceans, including dolphins and small whales. However the true porpoises from the family Phocoenidae are, in fact, well differentiated from other cetaceans. Dolphins have conical teeth and usually have a beak, while porpoises have spade-shaped teeth and no prominent beak. Porpoises also have relatively small flippers. There are currently seven species of porpoises, including the harbor porpoise (*Phocoena phocoena*), the most widespread and commonly seen of all the porpoises, the Dall's porpoise (*Phocoenoides dalli*) which has the reputation for being the fastest of all cetaceans, and the little known spectacled porpoise (*Phocoena dioptrica*).

With a body less than 1.5 m long, the vaquita, also known as the Gulf of California porpoise, is the smallest of all porpoises and of all cetaceans. It has one of the smallest geographic ranges, living only in the northern end of the Gulf of California, Mexico. It has also one of the smallest populations of all cetaceans. The vaquita, which means "little cow" in Spanish, was first described scientifically very recently in 1958, but today it is at great risk of extinction, as it is frequently entangled in fishing gear.

The fate of the vaquita reminds us that since the 1950s, the growth of modern fisheries and the use of destructive fishing methods have made the oceans and rivers of the world dangerous places for whales, dolphins and porpoises. Hundreds of thousands of them, possibly millions, die trapped in fishing nets every year.

Whales, dolphins, and porpoises amaze us by their extraordinary diversity. Their differences do not simply lie in their sizes, colors, shapes and habitats. They also display an astonishing diversity in their communication, social interactions, feeding methods and movements across the oceans. As a group, the cetaceans have accomplished some of the greatest achievements on earth. They have walked on land and evolved to become sea creatures. They have adapted to live in the darkest and the deepest of the oceans, in freezing waters as well as in warm, shallow waters in every part of the world. The more time we take to look into their world, the more we realize we are just starting to break the surface. The more we learn about whales, dolphins and porpoises, the more they fascinate us.

It is not known why whales breach, even though a variety of explanations have been proposed. It has been suggested that humpbacks breach to let other whales know they are nearby, stun fish while feeding, get rid of parasites, or show playfulness, fear, stress, aggression, or curiosity.

♠ Scientists do not really know why humpback whales engage in breaching. It is possible that such a dramatic behaviour may be used as a form of communication with other whales. Another explanation is that humpbacks breach to see what is above the water's surface.

The ventral surface of a humpback whale's head shows the barnacle-covered tubercles at the very tip, the protuding jaw plate at mid-line, and the ventral pleats extending down the length of the throat.

♠ Humpback whales have a range of display behaviours. Tail, pectoral fin and head displays may be used to signal location or to communicate various behavioural states such as aggression or competition.

♠ Humpback whales have a very broad head, with a single median ridge and a series of knobs, each containing a sensory hair.

The body of a humpback whale is black or dark gray dorsally and has significant amounts of white on the belly. The flippers are white on the ventral side and vary from all-white to mostly black on the dorsal surface. The ventral side of the flukes also varies from all-black to all-white. ➧

Humpback whales have the longest flippers of all cetaceans. Their flippers are up to one-third of their body length, and are used to herd fish, navigate, comfort their calves, and slap the surface of the water. ▶

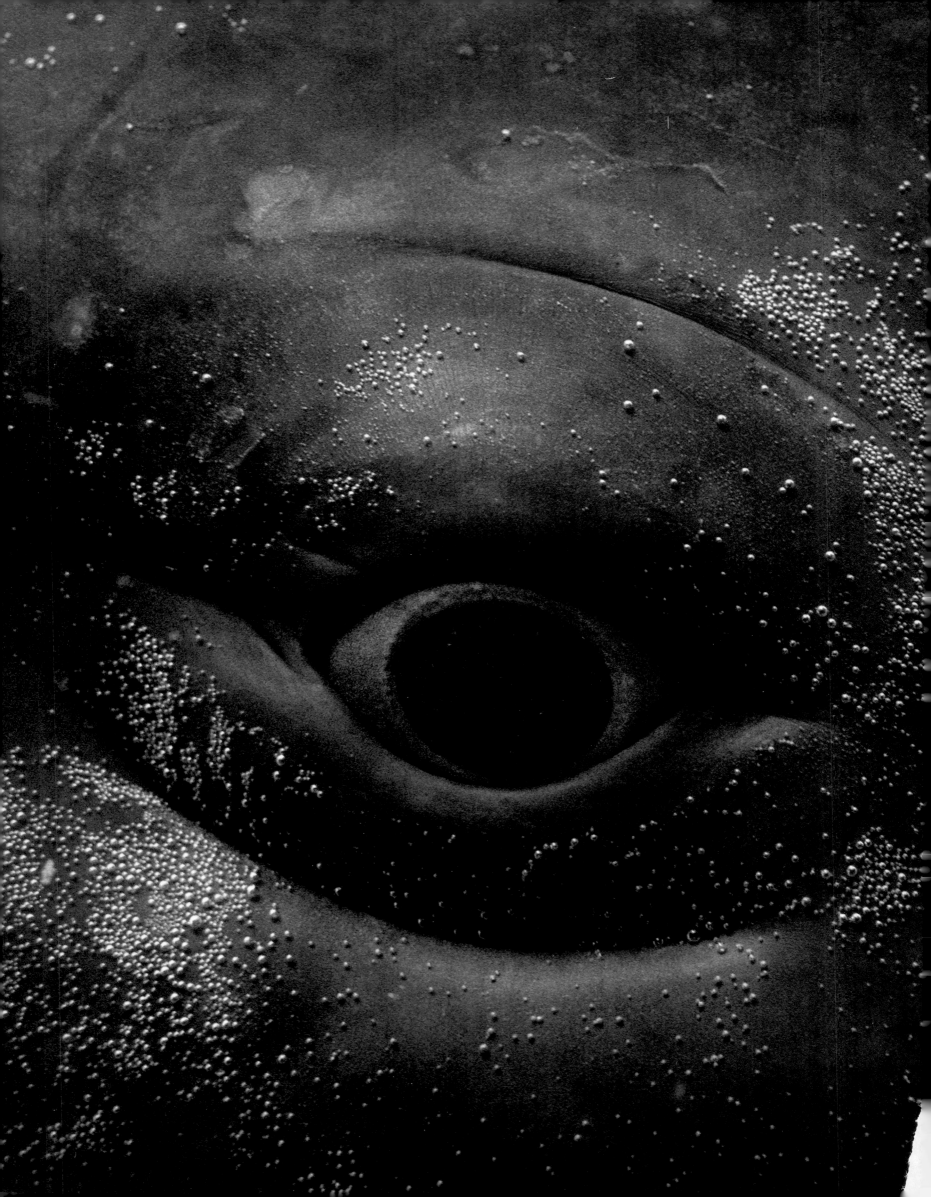

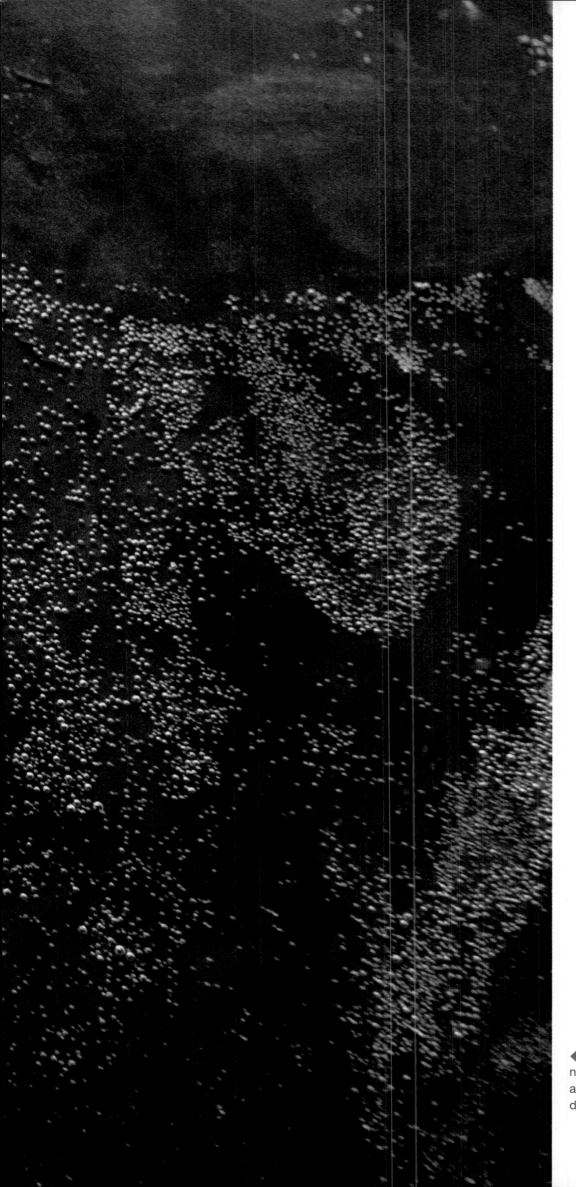

◀ The eye of a young sperm whale can see bioluminescent light produced by deep-sea creatures, such as squid, the sperm whale's favorite prey, that live in darkness at great ocean depths.

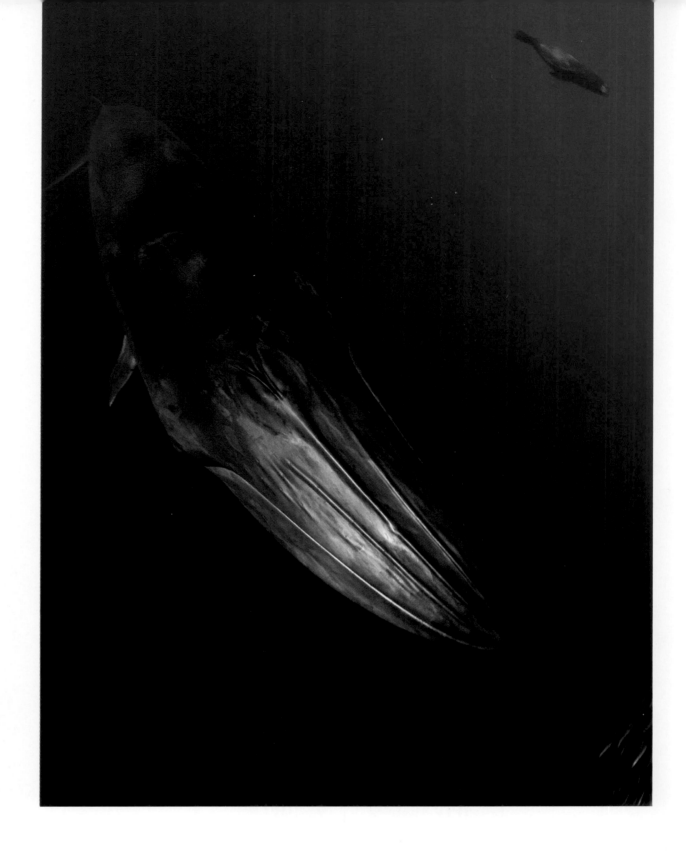

⬆ A Bryde's whale shows its streamlined and sleek body and head. Bryde's whales have three prominent ridges on the rostrum, which allows scientists to identify them. Other rorquals generally have only one.

A dwarf minke whale photographed underwater in Queensland, Australia, shows its color pattern asymmetry, typical of this species, and its sharply pointed head, characteristic of all minke whales. ➡

38-39 A 40' long Bryde's whale swims near a bait ball of mackerel and is joined by California sea lions. Bryde's whales primarily eat schooling fish such as pilchard, anchovy, sardine, mackerel, and herring. They are active lunge feeders, often changing direction abruptly when going after fast-moving fish.

⬆ The bubble blast of a dwarf minke whale is photographed in the Great Barrier Reef, Australia. In a bubble blast, an explosive cloud of bubbles is released from the whale's blowhole.

➡ A minke whale photographed in the Great Barrier Reef, Australia shows its sharply pointed, V-shaped head. The throat pleats are also visible. The minke whale's color is distinctive, dark gray dorsally and white beneath, with streaks of intermediate shades on the sides.

A juvenile gray whale is foraging in a kelp forest in California. Gray whales are found only in the North Pacific and are easy to recognize, with their scarred head covered in barnacles.

♠ This gray whale is foraging at the sea bottom. As a bottom feeder, the gray whale sifts the sediment for food, engulfing a mouthful of mud and water which it strains through the baleen. Its diet consists of bottom-dwelling invertebrates, particularly amphipod and isopod crustaceans, and segmented worms.

Dwarf minke whales are the smallest of the baleen whales. They have a characteristic white band on each fin that contrasts with a very dark grey fin tip. They are quite sleek in appearance. They are frequently reported in areas off the coasts of Australia, South America and South Africa. ➡

A southern right whale, photographed at close range underwater shows the numerous callosities characteristic of this species. The size and placement of these white patches are used to identify individual animals. ▶

◀ A southern right whale is swimming close to the surface. Southern right whales often seem slow and lumbering, but they can sometimes be surprisingly quick and active. They often breach, and slap their flippers and flukes on the surface.

50-51 A bowhead whale comes to the surface after feeding in Lancaster Sound, Canada. The bowhead whale is easily recognizable by its white chin and its massive head, which extends to almost one-third the length of the body. The baleen plates of bowhead whales can reach a length of more than 16 feet (5 m), the longest of any whale.

♠ As the largest toothed whale, the sperm whale is unlikely to be confused with any other species of cetacean. The body is somewhat compressed and the head is squarish and very large, extending to one-quarter to one-third of the total body length.

A sperm whale calf swims near the surface. Sperm whales are able to dive at great depths, but the calves cannot follow their mothers and are often looked after by other female sperm whales while the mothers forage at depth. ➡

◆ A sperm whale descends vertically. Sperm whales are the greatest divers of the ocean and can reach depths of up to 2 miles (3 km) below the surface. They generally stay submerged for 40 minutes but can stay underwater for up to two hours. They dive deep in search of deepwater squid.

↟ The body surface of sperm whales tends to be wrinkled behind the head and on the sides. Their flippers are short, but wide and spatulate. The flukes are broad and triangular with rounded tips.

♠ A group of pygmy killer whales swim in Hawaii, displaying most of the species' identifying characteristics. Little is known about pygmy killer whales, as they are rarely encountered. In Hawaii, they show high fidelity to specific islands.

These false killer whales swimming in Hawaii show their long, slender, cigar-shaped bodies. False killer whales are very social and are typically encountered in groups of 10 to 60 animals. This is one of the most common species involved in cetacean mass strandings. In one case, more than 800 animals stranded together.

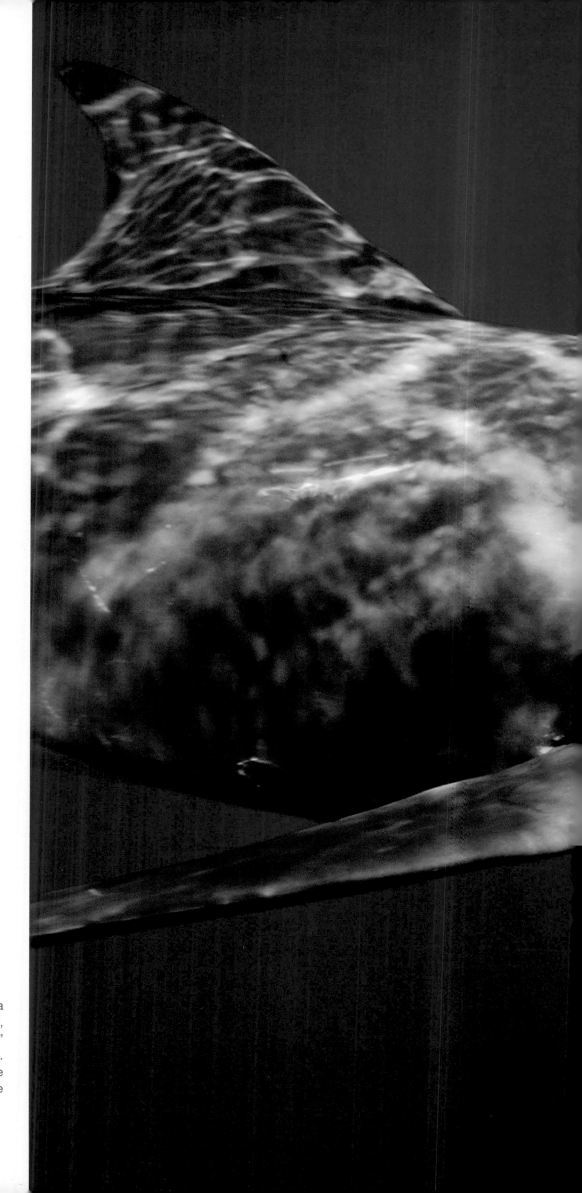

A pygmy killer whale photographed in Hawaii offers a good look of its rounded head, prominent dorsal fin, and long tapered flippers. As with other "blackfish," the body appears mostly dark with some white areas. The pygmy killer whale is often confused with the false killer whale and the melon-headed whale, which are similar in general appearance. ◆

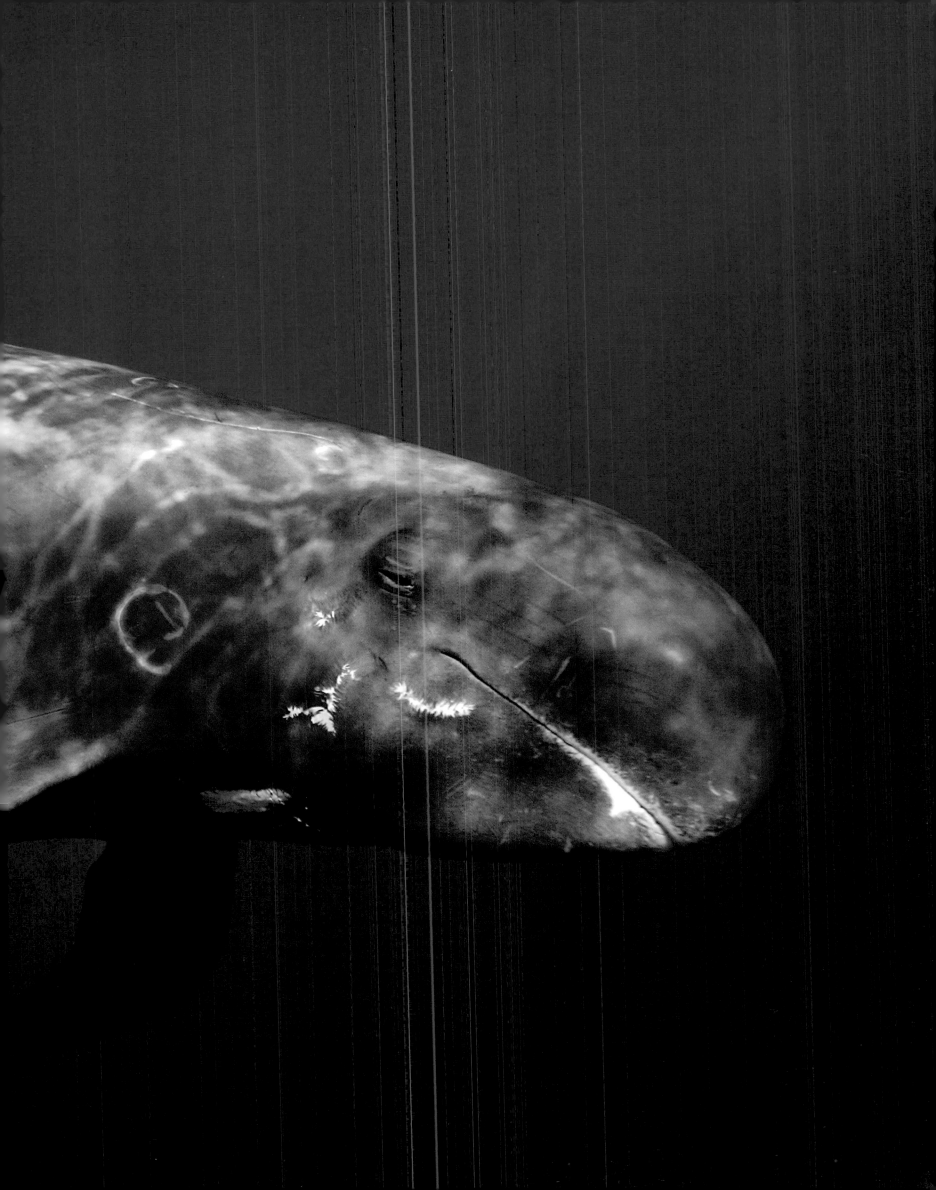

A false killer whale is swimming above a sandy sea bed in Subic Bay, Luzon, Philippines. False killer whales are lively, fast-swimming cetaceans, often leaping high into the air and making rapid turns underwater. ▶

⬆ False killer whales are known to behave aggressively toward other small cetaceans, and have even been observed chasing and attacking dolphins and large whales, such as humpback whales and even sperm whales. They also eat large fish such as mahi-mahi and tuna.

A false killer whale shows its sharp teeth. Each jaw contains 7 to 12 pairs of large conical teeth, which are round in cross-section. False killer whales need good teeth to hunt a wide array of prey. ▶

64-65 A killer whale breaches in Glacier Bay, Alaska. A breach occurs when a whale leaps out of the water, exposing two-thirds or more of its body. The iconic killer whale is one of the most universally recognized marine species, unmistakable even when it is not breaching.

A killer whale advancing in the water is showing its head and dorsal fin. The impressively tall, triangular dorsal fin of a male killer whale can reach a remarkable height of 6 feet (1.8 m). Biologists can identify individual killer whales based on distinctive features of each animal's dorsal fin and saddle-patch markings. ▶

◆ Killer whales are among the most acrobatic cetaceans. They exhibit a variety of behaviors while undertaking their daily activities. They often breach, spyhop, and slap the surface with their flukes or flippers. They exhibit varied responses to vessels, ranging from indifference to curiosity.

♠ Spyhopping is a behavior where a whale raises its head out of the water, probably to have a look above the surface. Many whales share this behavior. Orcas have good vision both above and below the water.

⬆ A killer whale performs a spectacular breach. Breaches may take place at any time when a group is active and are exhibited by orcas of all ages. Sometimes the same whale will breach several times in a row.

⬇ Two killer whales engage in impressive aerial displays. The functions of these acrobatic behaviors are uncertain, and probably vary with each situation.

▲ A killer whale photographed near the surface of the water shows its unmistakable black-and-white color pattern. The lower jaw, undersides of the flukes and the ventral surface are white. The rest of the body is black, except for a light gray saddle patch behind the dorsal fin. The orca's distinctive color pattern may serve to confuse predators and facilitate social interaction.

A killer whale shows its large, rounded flippers. Flippers can grow to lengths of up to 6.5 feet (2 m). Killer whales rest, sometimes for hours at a time, by floating or swimming slowly near the surface.

◀ A group of male narwhals gather at the Arctic ice edge to eat cod. Most pods of narwhals consist of 2 to 10 individuals, but there is evidence that these groups are often part of larger, scattered herds of hundreds or even thousands of animals, particularly in the summer.

Lancaster Sound, Nunavut, Canada. The male narwhal has two teeth. The one on the right normally remains invisible, but the one on the left grows to a remarkable length. It pierces the animal's upper lip, and develops into a long tusk. The tusk can grow up to 9 feet (2.7 m) long. ▶

78-79 A narwhal photographed underwater shows its full body. Young narwhals are uniformly gray to brownish gray. As they age, they darken and white mottling appears. They appear spotted and the belly becomes light gray to white with some dark mottling. Lightening continues as the animal ages. Older animals often appear nearly white.

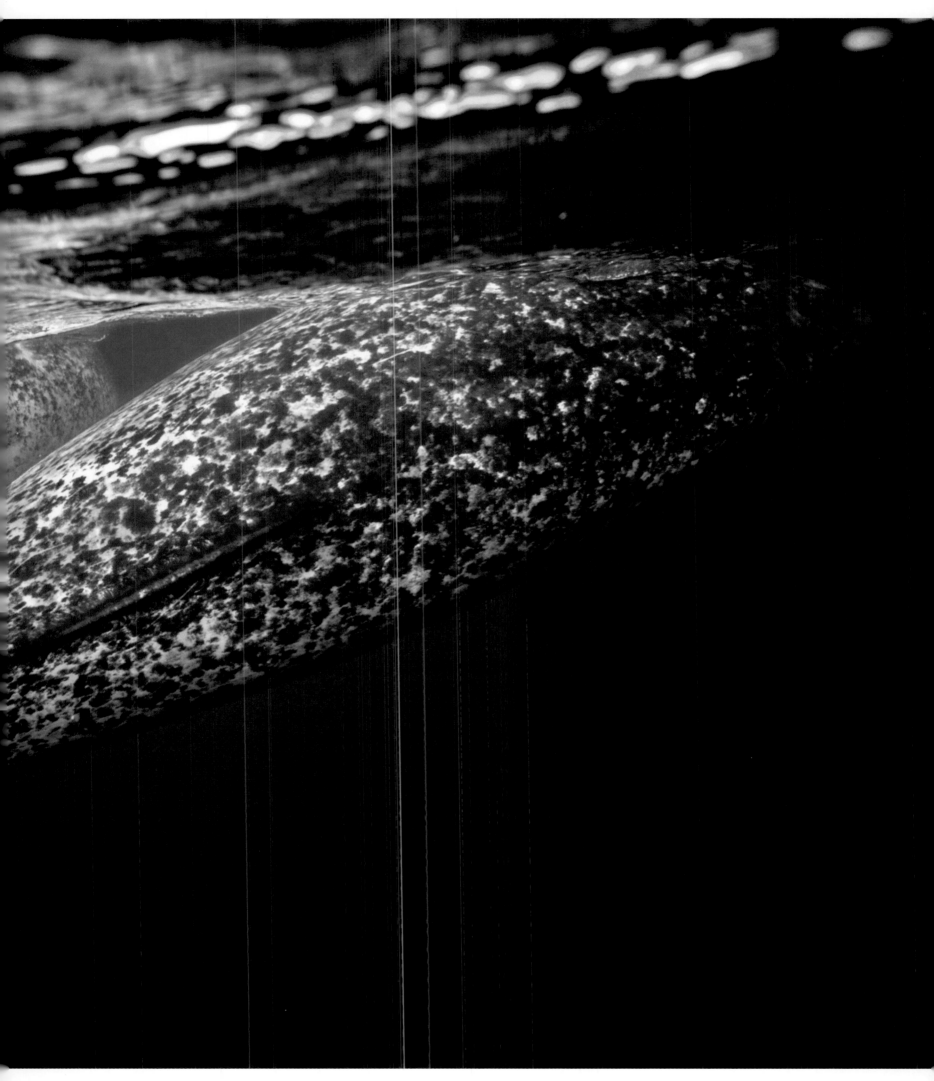

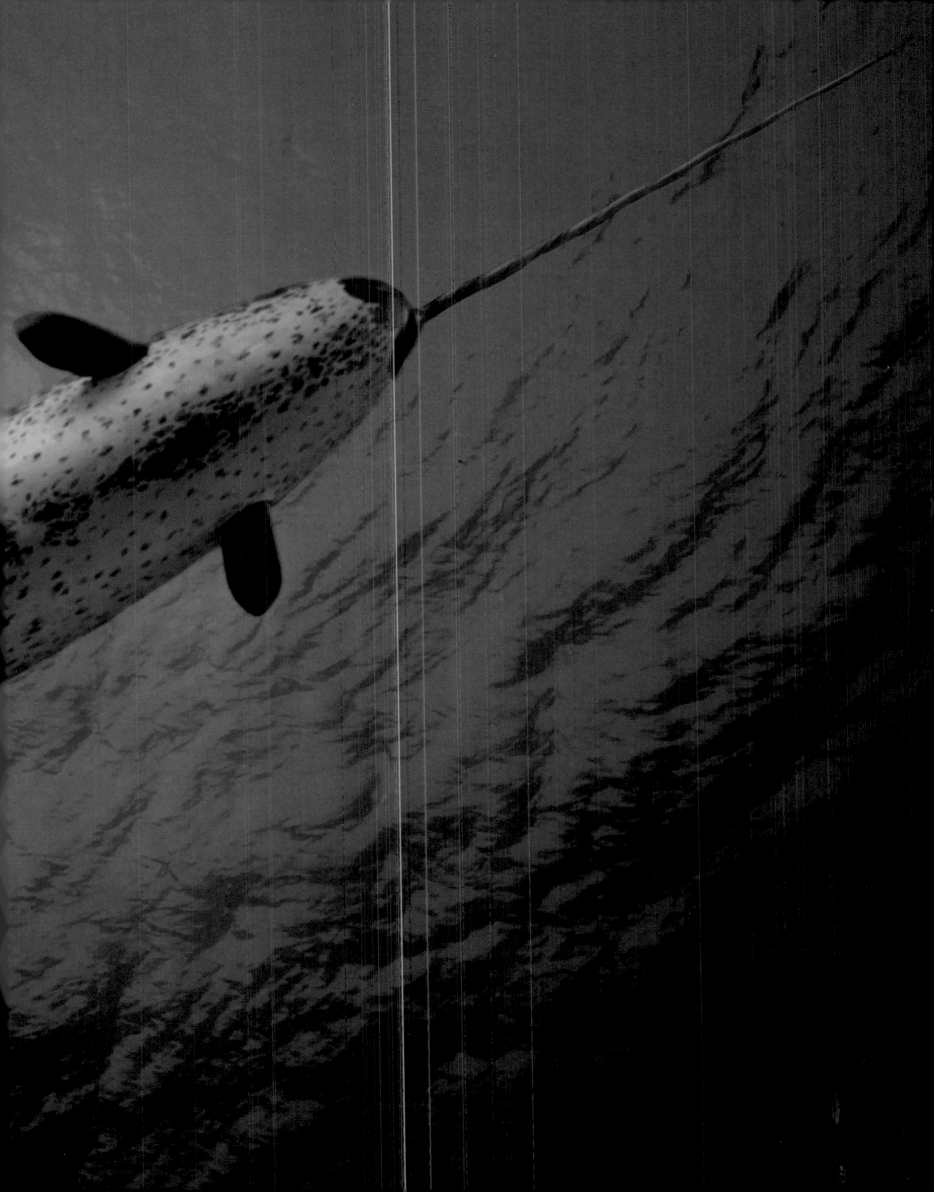

◀ The tusk of male narwhals has long been a source of scientific controversy. It appears to be used in male competition for females, and perhaps as a display for attracting females. Male narwhals have been observed sparring with their tusks above water.

A group of beluga whales swim in the Arctic ice. Getting trapped in shifting ice is an ever-present danger for this species. Polar bears may wait at breathing holes in the ice, and pull beluga whales from the water as they surface to breathe.

♠ Belugas are sociable whales and are often encountered in groups of 5 to 10 animals, although they may form larger seasonal gatherings of thousands of animals. They spend much time at the surface, often off shallow coasts and river mouths. They are capable of maneuvering through partially ice-covered water.

A beluga whale spyhops in the Canadian high Arctic, showing its distinctive bulbous head, short beak, flexible neck, thick lips, and expressive face. This animal has numerous rake marks that could have been the result of attacks from killer whales or polar bears. ▶

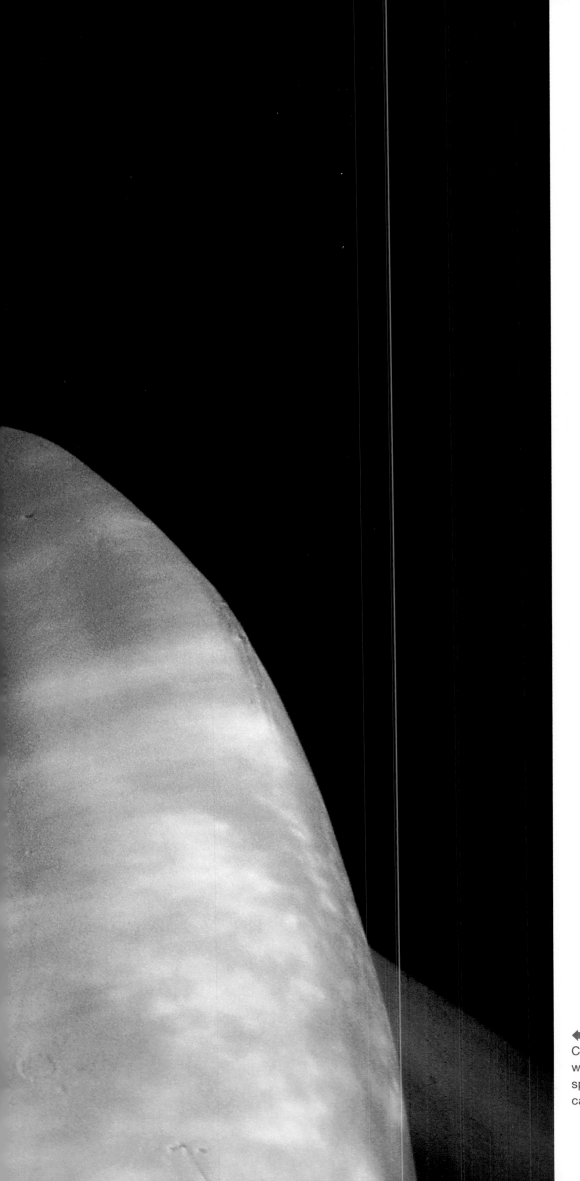

◀ A group of beluga whales photographed in the Churchill River, Manitoba, Canada, show their all white body color which is so characteristic of this species. Belugas may dive for up to 25 minutes, and can reach depths of over 2,600 feet (800 m).

◀ Eight common bottlenose dolphins jump side by side. They are very active, particularly when feeding and socializing, and often slap the water with their flukes, leap, and perform other impressive aerial behaviors.

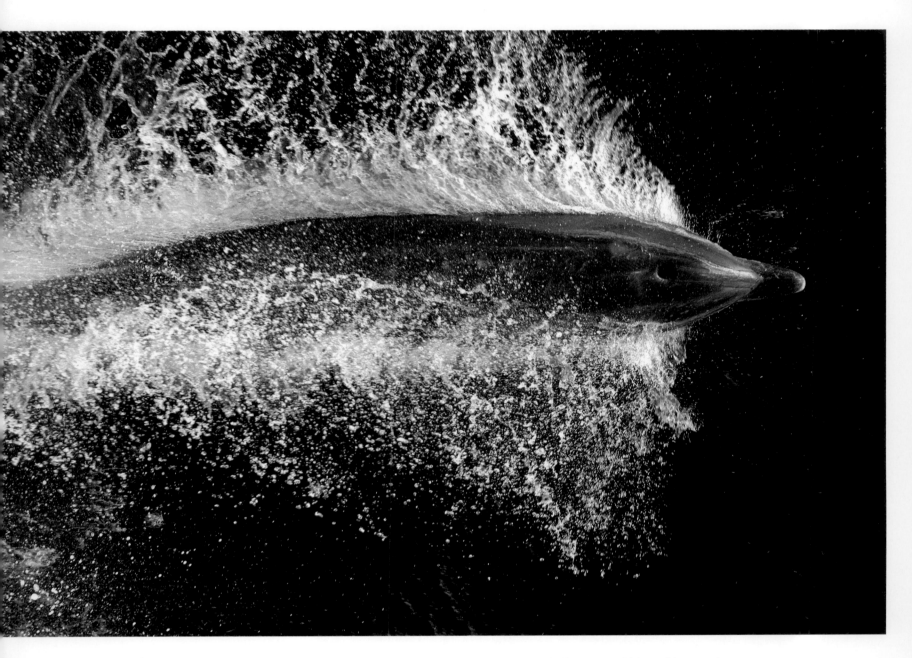

♠ A common bottlenose dolphin is breaking the surface. Bottlenose dolphins are avid bowriders and may perform acrobatic leaps while riding. They also sometimes ride the waves produced by large whales.

A common bottlenose dolphin, just at the surface, shows its robust body shape, and its curved flippers, pointed at the tips. There is considerable variation in the way bottlenose dolphins look depending on where they live. Offshore animals tend to be larger and darker in color, with smaller flippers, than their inshore counterparts. ▶

Dolphins produce clicks and squeals when they vocalize. On occasion, they expel clouds of bubbles through their blowholes, such as this Atlantic spotted dolphin. Some researchers believe that these underwater bubbles may be an expression of surprise or disquiet.

An Atlantic spotted dolphin leaves a stream of bubbles as it whistles underwater. Dolphins use whistles and other sounds to identify themselves, communicate with group members and to find food.

A common bottlenose dolphin swims in shallow waters in Belize. Bottlenose dolphins live in tropical to temperate waters worldwide, close to shore and far out to sea. They can be curious and often approach swimmers and boats. ▶

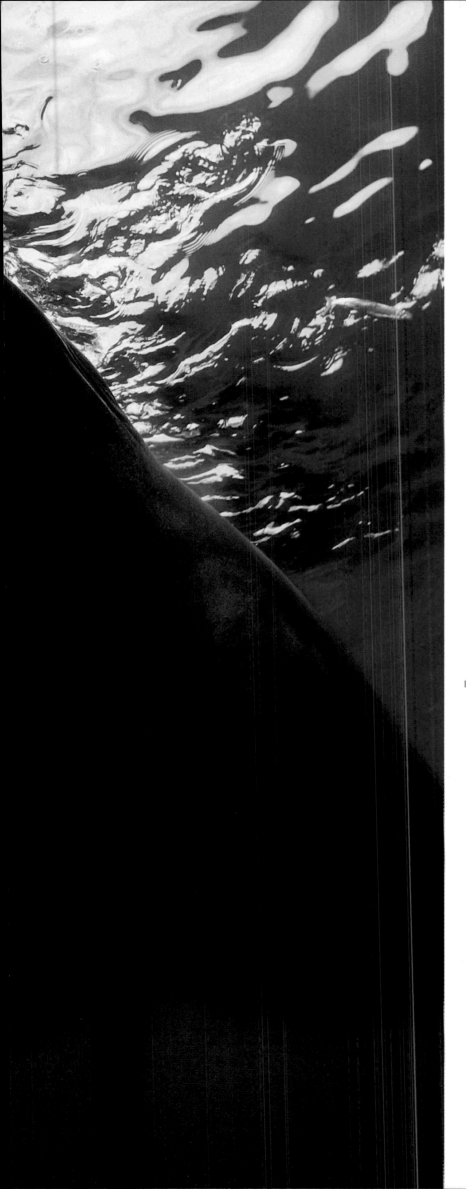

FROM SMALL FISH EATER TO SEA LION HUNTER

THE DIVERSITY OF CETACEAN DIETS

FROM SMALL FISH EATER TO SEA LION HUNTER

THE DIVERSITY OF CETACEAN DIETS

The largest animal on the planet, the blue whale, eats some of the smallest organisms on Earth, shrimp-like creatures called krill. During the feeding season, blue whales can eat up to four tons of krill per day. How an animal weighing more 100 tons and growing up to 100 feet (30 m) long came to survive on tiny shrimp that are just a couple of inches long is one of nature's most fascinating mysteries. Equally fascinating is how killer whales in Patagonia, Argentina, have developed a unique hunting strategy to catch sea lion pups by launching themselves onto the beach.

The dining habits of whales, dolphins and porpoises are remarkably varied and continue to challenge the human mind. Whether they dine on krill, fish, or marine mammals, they all have evolved specialized techniques and anatomic features to get food. Some eat alone, others hunt in groups. Some use their teeth to catch prey, while others rely on baleen plates to filter food.

Baleen whales are the largest animals in the sea, and they feed on some of the smallest. They are part of a short food chain, which begins with phytoplankton that floats in the upper layer of the ocean. Phytoplankton synthesizes sunlight into energy and in turn is consumed by zooplankton. The zooplankton and phytoplankton are eaten by small fishes, and together these links in the food chain are consumed by the whales. Krill is the staple food of baleen whales, but they also capture small fish such as capelin, herring, pilchard and other tiny marine organisms using hundreds of baleen plates that hang from their upper jaws. The baleen plates, called "whalebone" by early whalers, are actually made of keratin, the same ingredient found in fingernails. Baleen is an elaborate filtration system in the mouth that looks like a comb and serves to filter small prey from large volumes of seawater. The inner surface of the baleen features a dense mat of hair, which serves as a strainer. The length of baleen plates depends on the whale's feeding method, from up to 13 feet (4 m)-long plates for the bowhead whale to the short plates of the grey whale which are only about 10 inches (25 cm) long. In their summer feeding grounds, baleen whales eat all day along. Blue whales may consume as many as 40 million krill each day, and need to eat as much as they can, because when they start migrating to their breeding grounds, they will fast and live off stored fat.

Baleen whales catch their dinner in different ways. Some skim at the surface, others strain food out of the water, and still others sift food from the ocean floor. The rorquals, which includes fin, blue and humpback whales, are "gulpers." While foraging for krill, the whale opens its mouth and takes a high-speed dive, called a lunge, creating powerful drag comparable to a race car driver opening a parachute. The drag that is generated forces the water into the mouth. The whale then looks like a giant tadpole, with its throat grooves that expand like the pleats of a skirt and increase the capacity of the mouth. After expanding with each mouthful, the throat plects contract and in less than a minute the water is forced out of the mouth while prey remains trapped on the inner surface of the baleen. The volume of water engulfed and filtered during each lunge is larger than the whale's entire body.

Humpback whales have developed a special lunge feeding technique to obtain their meal, called "bubble netting." A whale slowly rises from below a school of prey such as herring or krill, swimming in an upward spiral around the prey, and releasing bubbles from its blowhole. These form a "net," causing prey to panic and converge into the circle of bubbles. Several whales then fly up through the curtain of bubbles with mouths open wide, and feast on the concentrated prey. Bubble nets vary in size and shape depending on which humpback whale is blowing the bubbles, how many whales are involved in the hunt, and what kind of fish they are hunting. Bubble netting requires the whales to work together, as one whale is producing bubbles and another is focused on herding the prey into the bubble net. This cooperative behaviour has been compared to a football team, and researchers have shown that individual whales choose who they want to bubble-net with.

While rorquals such as blue and humpback whales are gulpers, other baleen whales are "skimmers." Skim feeders such as the right whales and the bowhead whales graze through patches of surface-dwelling plankton with their mouths wide open and continuously filter prey as they slowly swim along near the surface. Both right whales and bowheads have very long baleen to filter large volumes of water. When enough food has accumulated on the baleen, the whales close their mouths and swallow the catch.

Grey whales have completely different dining habits. They are bottom feeders, and just like tractors in a field, they plow the seabed near the coast and seek out mud-dwelling invertebrates, leaving a plume of disturbed mud behind them as they forage along the bottom of the ocean. They filter the sediment through their baleen plates which have short, stiff fringes, good at straining out small crustaceans from the mud. Usually one side of the jaw is more worn, suggesting that the whales prefer to roll over onto one side to feed. Grey whales have adapted to harvest coastal invertebrates. They adjust their feeding techniques to the type of prey they are after, and they work as farmers, picking the best crops when they are in season.

Scientists do not exactly know why whales use different techniques to catch a meal, but they assume the animals try to be as efficient as possible and adapt their feeding strategies based on the location of the krill, just below the surface or in deeper waters, and how concen-

96-97 A Bryde's whale feeds on a bait ball of sardines, off Baja California, Mexico. Bryde's whales are gulp feeders that often lunge rapidly on their sides into schools of prey. Like other rorquals, they have unique adaptations for feeding on large quantities of small fish.

trated the prey is. Whales burn so many calories when they lunge feed that they typically look for the densest krill patches to maximize prey catch. For example, researchers have observed that blue whales cover great distances and move fast from one area to the next, searching for the places that have the most krill. They are so big that they cannot afford to waste energy snacking on small patches of krill; they need big, hearty meals.

How baleen whales detect large aggregations of prey, such as krill swarms or fish schools in a vast and changing ocean is still debated. Researchers have wondered whether the whales remember the best spots to catch a good meal from one year to the next or whether they simply roam the ocean until they hit a school of prey. One of the reasons blue whales have evolved to be the largest animals on the planet is that the energy cost of travelling declines as body size increases. Because blue whales are so big and have huge fat reserves, they can travel in the ocean for long periods of time searching for food, without expending too much energy. It is also probable that the whales use their auditory sense to locate krill swarms and schooling fish, which allows them to read environmental cues that lead them to the best dining tables in the ocean. Blue whales may be listening for ocean storms and subtle changes in the ambient noise created by thick krill patches. They may also use their low-frequency voices to broadcast to others where the food is.

Sharing information is of advantage to the whales because the food is so sparsely distributed that it ultimately benefits them to announce the presence of a food patch to others. Unfortunately, the ocean is becoming noisier and noisier because of increased boat traffic, oil and gas exploration, and urban development along the coastline. These human activities impact the whales' acoustic habitat, interfering with their ability to hear each other and effectively detect food.

When it comes to catching a meal, toothed whales have a completely different diet from baleen whales. They eat fish, squid, octopus, large crustaceans, and marine mammals. Toothed whales display an astonishing variety of techniques to catch food, using echolocation, communication, and highly sophisticated group hunting strategies. Behaviour patterns of many species depend largely on what they eat. Some species laze and socialize during the day and hunt at night, while others feed during daylight and relax at night. Their teeth and snouts are adapted to the prey they eat. Most dolphins use their conical, pointed teeth to grasp slippery prey such as fish, which they swallow whole. Some species like long-beaked common dolphins have 47 to 67 pairs of small sharp conical teeth that are useful for catching small schooling fish. Pilot whales have only 40 to 48 teeth and do not need many teeth because they feed mostly on squid. Most beaked whales have no functional teeth and actually use suction to capture squid and fish. Among species that subsist largely or entirely on squid are the sperm and beaked whales. These squid feeders exhibit a number of adaptations for employing the tongue as a piston and sucking squid into their mouths.

The ocean is a big place, and one may wonder how toothed whales find food. Luckily they have a sophisticated detection mechanism, called echolocation, a natural sonar that allows them to track prey even when it is dark or the water is murky. Some river dolphins depend so heavily on echolocation that they have almost lost the use of their eyes. Toothed whales send out high-frequency signals and listen to the echoes as the sounds bounce off objects in the environment. From the echo, a cetacean can determine the size, shape, texture, distance, and movements of objects. The greater the distance an object is located from the cetacean, the longer it takes for the echo to return. This evolutionary adaptation allows cetaceans to "see" their environment through sound and has contributed to their hunting success and survival.

In addition to echolocation, toothed whales may use vision to discover and approach prey. For example many squid are bioluminescent, and it is possible that sperm whales use their bioluminescence to locate the squid in the darkness of deep ocean waters.

Dolphins are extremely efficient predators. Not only do they use echolocation to hunt for prey, but also speed, communication and cooperation. They use a wide array of behaviours to pursue and capture prey. Their techniques depend on a variety of factors such as the attributes of the habitat they are feeding in, the type of fish they are after, and how deep they are hunting. Bottlenose dolphins can be very creative and have a broad range of foraging behaviours to catch different prey species. Calves learn these tricks from their mothers. For example, dolphins stir up sediment to trap prey, chase fish onto mud banks and beaches, stun fish in the shallows by whacking them with their flukes, and beach hunt. In Shark Bay, Western Australia, studies have shown that bottlenose dolphins use more than a dozen different hunting tactics to catch dinner. Some of them even have a technique called "sponging." They pick up marine sponges, wear them over their beaks and use them as foraging tools to probe into the seafloor for fish.

Some dolphins have also adapted to human activities and follow fishing boats to get discarded fish. They even work cooperatively with net fishers to catch fish. In Laguna, Brazil, bottlenose dolphins have been working with local fishermen to herd fish into their nets for more than 150 years. They are rewarded by being given part of the catch.

Dolphins often work in groups to increase hunting efficiency and carefully plan coordinated attacks. For example, they drive fish towards the surface, herd them into a dense, tight ball and then take turns to dash in and feed. Several species of dolphins engage in this communal hunting behaviour, such as dusky dolphins, bottlenose dolphins, common dolphins, clymene dolphins, and Atlantic spotted dolphins. In South Carolina, bottlenose dolphins encircle schools of fish and drive them toward the shallows in rivers and estuaries. Eventually the frightened fish run aground and the dolphins follow them, temporarily beaching themselves to pick the fish off the shore, and then wriggle to get themselves back into the water. In Cedar Key, Florida, group-hunting bottlenose dolphins practice division of labour during coordinated foraging, with one individual dolphin assuming the role of "driver" and other dolphins in the group acting as the "barrier" to the fish. The "driver" lifts its tail out of the water and vigorously slaps it against the water surface, herding fish towards the tightly grouped barrier. Fish leap into the air and are captured by the driver and barrier dolphins. The athletic, acrobatic spinner dolphins in Hawaii are also known for their elegant teamwork, displaying perfect synchronization when they engage in a nocturnal "dance" to first enclose their prey and then dart into the circle of confused fish in organized pairs to feed, before backing out and letting the next pair in line take their turn.

Orcas or killer whales are widely distributed across the world's oceans, yet they display highly specialized hunting techniques. They are remarkable predators and hunt an astonishing array of marine species, ranging from dozens of varieties of fish, seals, sea lions and sea otters to great whales such as humpback and grey whales. At Punta Norte, along the eastern coast of Argentina, they beach themselves to hunt sea lions and elephant seal pups. This risky strategy requires high skill because the orcas can easily become fatally stranded if their plan is not carefully executed. One killer whale in a group often assumes primary responsibility for hunting, first patiently patrolling the shoreline from a distance while remaining silent as not to alert prey. The orca looks for the best spot suited to a sudden sneak attack, and strikes with speed and agility when it identifies an unsuspecting pup. As it reaches the shallows, the orca thrusts its body almost entirely out of water onto the beach and seizes the hapless pup in its jaws, shaking it vigorously, and slides back into the sea with the next wave. Older killer whales teach this method to young ones, often tossing a sea lion to juveniles for them to practice.

Off the coast of Norway, killer whale populations are known to congregate seasonally to pursue vast shoals of overwintering herring. In this technique, orcas join forces and begin to swim rapidly under and around a school of herring. The fish panic and get closer until they form a single, densely packed ball. The orcas gradually chase the school towards the surface and further disorient their prey. Some of the killer whales slap their tail flukes against the surface, others dive upside down under the fish, preventing them from escape. Individual whales take turns swimming into the densely packed herring to feed, often delivering a powerful blow to the herring with their tail flukes to stun the fish.

Monterey Bay, along the central California coast, is a prime hunting zone for transient killer whales, which prey on grey whale calves travelling with their mothers during late spring on their northward migration. The killer whales form small groups of five to ten individuals to surround a mother/calf pair. As much as six hours may pass from the initial attack to the kill with ramming, biting, pulling on the pectoral fins, and attempts to separate the mother from the calf. During this period the mother and calf try to dash for the safety of shallow water. The mother grey whale will actively defend her calf, interposing her own body between the killer whale and the calf, and often rolling belly up to allow her calf to get on top of her for brief periods of safety. If the killer whales are successful in driving away the mother, the calf is swiftly drowned and feeding commences. Similarly, in the remote waters off Unimak Island/False Pass area in Alaska's eastern Aleutian Islands, killer whales congregate and use team work to hunt migrating grey whales.

While some orcas have a diverse diet, others specialize in a particular prey. Among the killer whale populations off Vancouver Island in British Columbia, Canada and off Washington state, USA, the resident killer whales exclusively feed on fish, and the transient orcas feed on a variety of marine mammals such as harbour seals, Steller sea lions and porpoises. The transients are silent most of the time and rely on stealth to find their prey. They travel in small groups, quietly listening for the marine mammals they are hunting in order to catch them by surprise. Conversely, the resident killer whales are highly vocal when they hunt for fish. They feed on specific runs of salmon, and particularly enjoy Chinook salmon for dinner.

The specialized diet of the orcas of the Pacific Northwest has put them at considerable risk because many stocks of Pacific salmon have declined significantly due to overfishing, habitat degradation, dam building, urban development, fish farms, forestry and agricultural practices. In periods of Chinook salmon declines, the mortality rate of orcas climbs. In particular, a sharp decline in Chinook abundance during the late 1990s was associated with southern resident killer whale mortality rates more than twice what was expected. These killer whales are not the only ones impacted by changes in food availability. In other regions, climate change affects cetaceans' food source such as krill, and whales are forced to work harder and travel greater distances to feed.

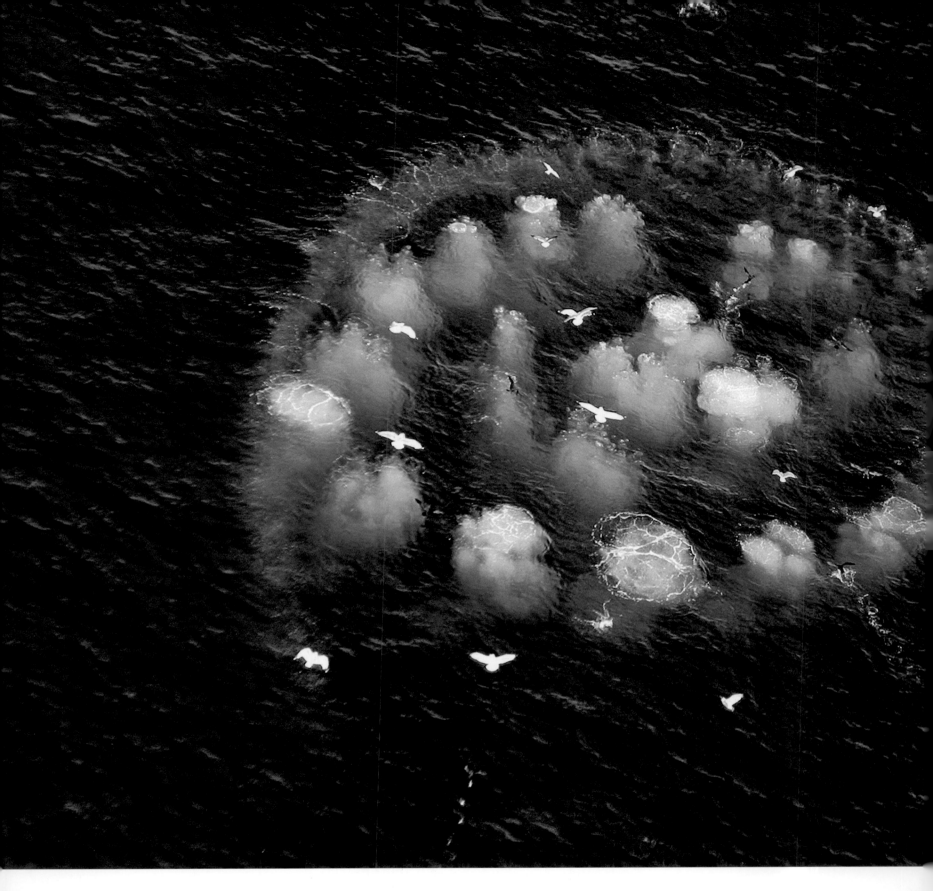

♠ Humpback whales are cooperatively bubble net feeding in the Gulf of Maine, USA. Humpbacks employ a surprising variety of techniques to herd and capture their prey of krill and small fish. They show an elaborate form of gulp feeding, called bubble netting, where they use curtains of bubbles to concentrate prey.

In bubble netting, humpback whales slowly swim in an upward spiral from below a school of prey, expelling a circle of bubbles from their blowholes.

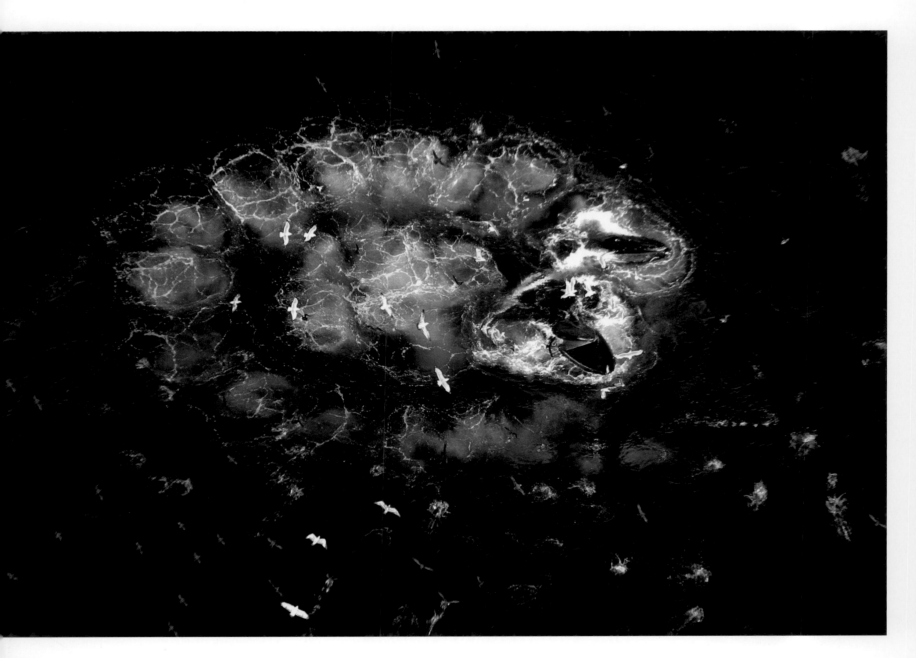

⬆ The bubbles form a "net" causing prey to panic and converge. The humpback whales then rise through the concentrated prey, mouths open wide. The whales surge towards the sky then fall back with a thunderous crash.

After engulfing a mouthful of prey-laden water, a humpback whale constricts its throat pleats, forcing the food and water upwards and back into its mouth. The engulfed water is filtered out, leaving food captured on the fringed edges of the baleen. The whale then swallows the food with its tongue. ⮞

Humpback whales feed in Frederick Sound, Alaska. Humpbacks have a diverse diet, feeding largely on krill and a wide variety of small schooling fish such as herring, sand lance, mackerel, sardines, anchovies, and capelin. They are one of the few species of baleen whales that use cooperative feeding techniques. ▶

◀ The gulp of a feeding humpback whale exposes the bony pink roof of its mouth, from which grows the food-entrapping sieve of baleen. Humpback whales have 270 to 400 baleen plates on each side of the upper jaw.

◀ A group of humpback whales lunge feed at the surface in southern Alaska. The size of a feeding group of humpback whales may depend on the size of the swarm on which they are feeding. Seabirds often congregate nearby in the hope of catching part of the meal.

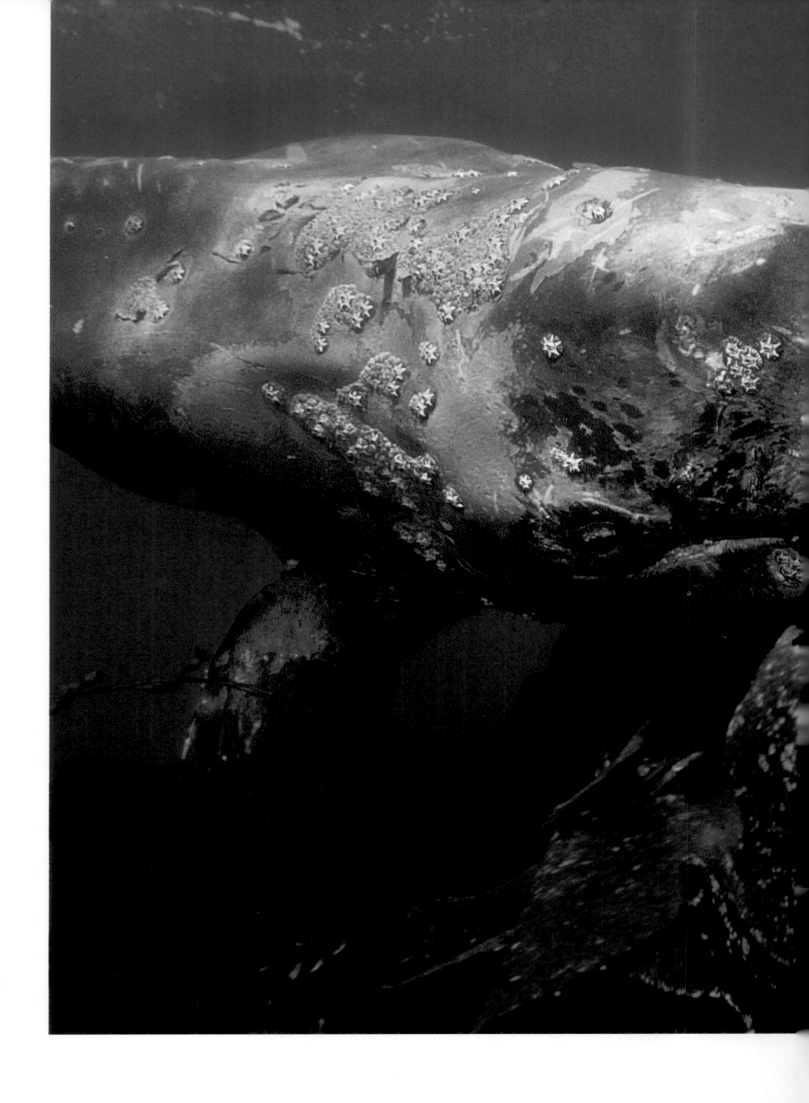

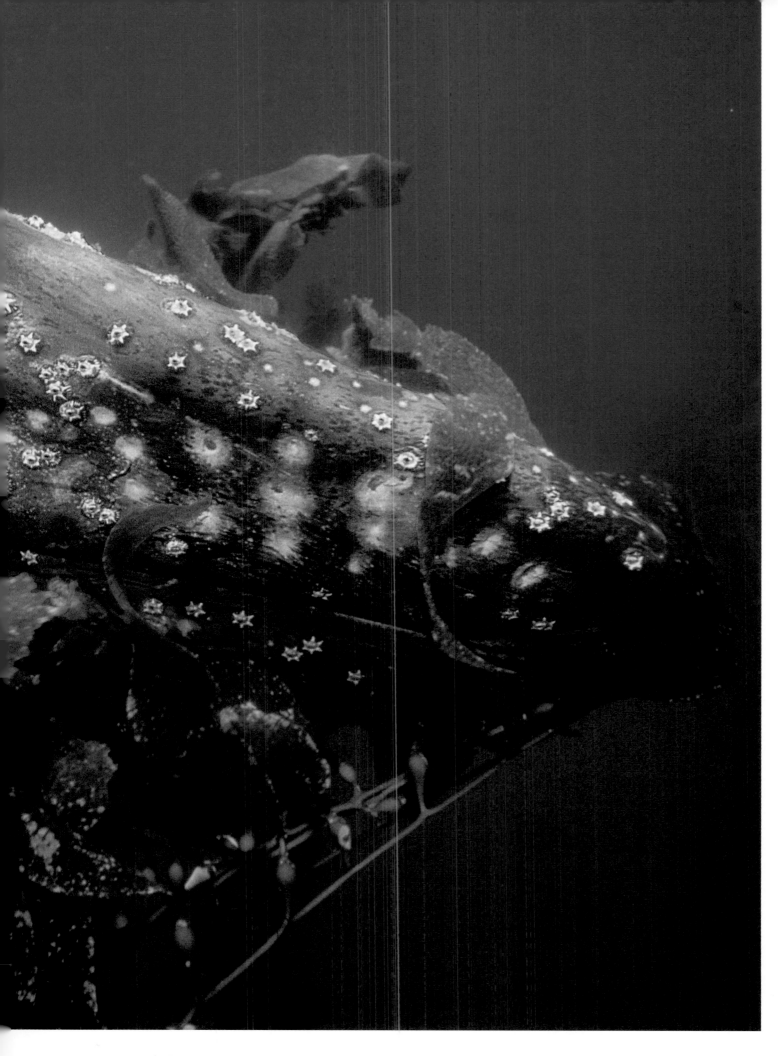

↑ Gray whales are highly adaptable feeders. They retrieve amphipods living in the seafloor sediment, filter plankton in open water, and eat herring roe. During mass spawning, herring lay eggs by the millions on kelp fronds. Gray whales harvest the spawn by clamping the kelp fronds in their mouths and pulling them through their baleen, stripping off the eggs.

⬆ A gray whale bottom feeds in the sands of San Ignacio Lagoon, Baja California, Mexico. Scouring the shallows, a gray whale leaves a visible trail of mud. It will either feed as it burrows through the silt or simply disturb the mud in order to flush out tiny animals, returning later to swallow them.

A gray whale shows its open mouth in San Ignacio Lagoon, Baja California, Mexico. Gray whales have short baleen plates that are 2 to 16 inches (5 to 40 cm) long with coarse bristles. Usually one or the other side of the jaw is more worn, suggesting that they prefer to roll over onto one side to feed. ▶

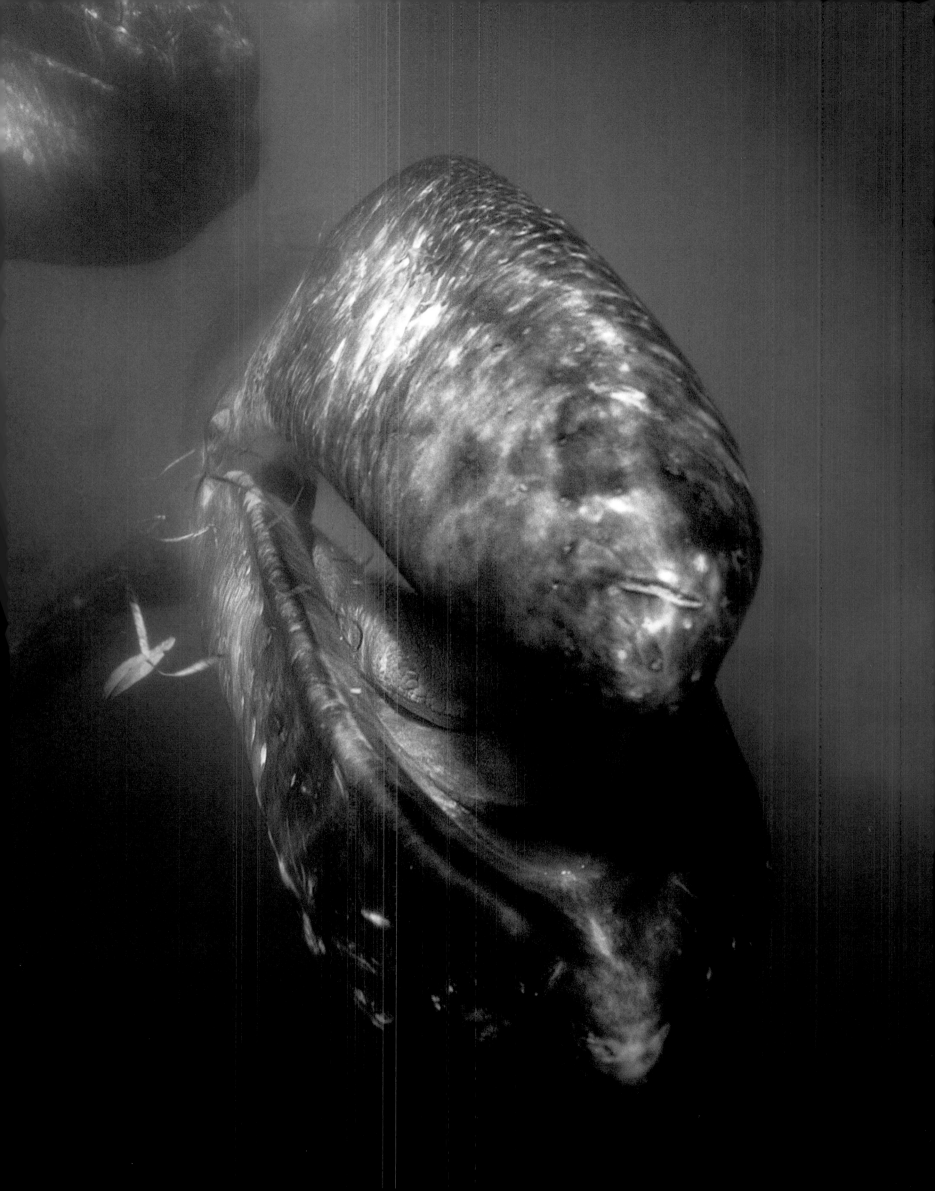

♠ A Bryde's whale charges through a bait ball of sardines, in Baja California, Mexico. The Bryde's whale is the least known of the large baleen whales, and the most unusual one because it does not seem to migrate long distances between feeding and breeding grounds every year. Instead, it stays in warm to temperate waters year round.

120-121 After expanding with each mouthful, the Bryde's whale's muscular throat pleats contract and the tongue moves forward, forcing water from the mouth out through the filtering baleen. Once the whale has squeezed out the water, it swallows the food, possibly with the aid of its mobile, muscular tongue.

A Bryde's whale shows its throat pleats while feeding on sardines. A feature shared by all rorquals, these folds of skin and muscle are what allow the throat and mouth to expand greatly when the whale engulfs prey-laden water.

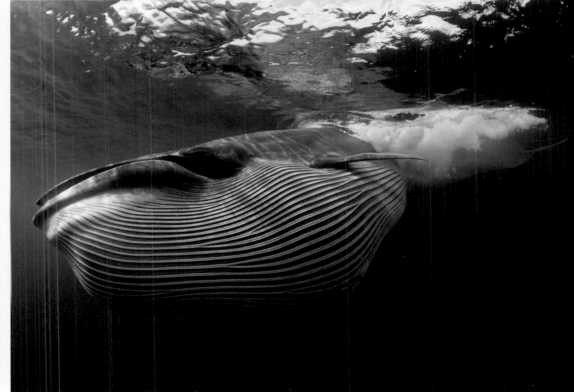

⬇ Rorquals such as this Bryde's whale feed on Pacific sardines, in addition to several other prey species. Common prey for Bryde's whales include pilchard, anchovies, sardines, mackerel, and herring, but they also take squid, krill, pelagic red crabs, and other invertebrates.

♠ Sei's and Bryde's whales are so similar that it was not until the early 1900's that whalers realized they were hunting two different species. The Sei whale has 32 to 60 throat grooves, while the Bryde's has 40 to 50 throat grooves, as revealed on this photograph of a Bryde's whale feeding on Pacific sardines.

🔺 Gulp feeders such as this Bryde's whale often concentrate prey to make it easier to capture, by herding a swarm against the water's surface or the shore. Lunging towards the surface, they engulf prey as they go, or they roll on their sides just below the surface and make rapid turns through the prey.

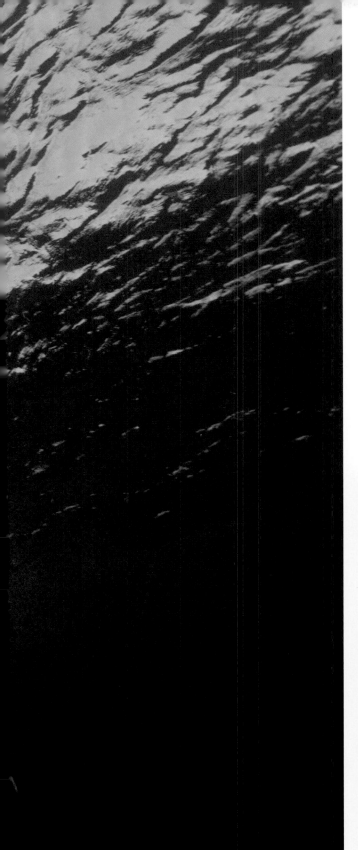

Schooling fish are alert, active, quick animals, and feeding rorquals, such as this Bryde's whale going after a school of Pacific sardines, need to move fast in order to capture them.

The sardine run along the east coast of South Africa is a spectacular phenomenon. Numerous species of marine mammals take advantage of this bountiful food supply, including Bryde's whales, observed here moving rapidly and plunging through the bait ball of sardines.

♠ This Bryde's whale is swimming behind a huge bait ball of Pacific sardines and is joined in the feeding frenzy by California sea lions. While feeding, the Bryde's whale usually displays a regular up-and-down pattern, frequently arching its back quite high and diving from 5 to 15 minutes.

128-129 The killer whale is one of nature's supreme predators and displays a variety of specialized hunting techniques. This orca launches itself out of the water on a beach in Valdes Peninsula, Patagonia, Argentina, in quest of unsuspecting sea lion pups splashing in the shallows.

During such attacks, killer whales grab sea lion pups in their impressive jaws, using a sophisticated hunting technique honed to perfection. The orcas may ram or strike their prey with their tail flukes for an hour or more before it is drowned and eaten. ▶

132-133 Adult orcas teach their young how to beach themselves to snatch the naive sea lion pups. However, this hunting technique is risky and requires a great deal of skill. Orcas show the juveniles how to wriggle off the beach if they become stranded.

134-135 Each year the great sardine run along the east coast of South Africa is a dynamic and complex event that attracts thousands of marine animals, including copper sharks, Cape gannets, predatory fish, and the common dolphins that are shown in this photograph.

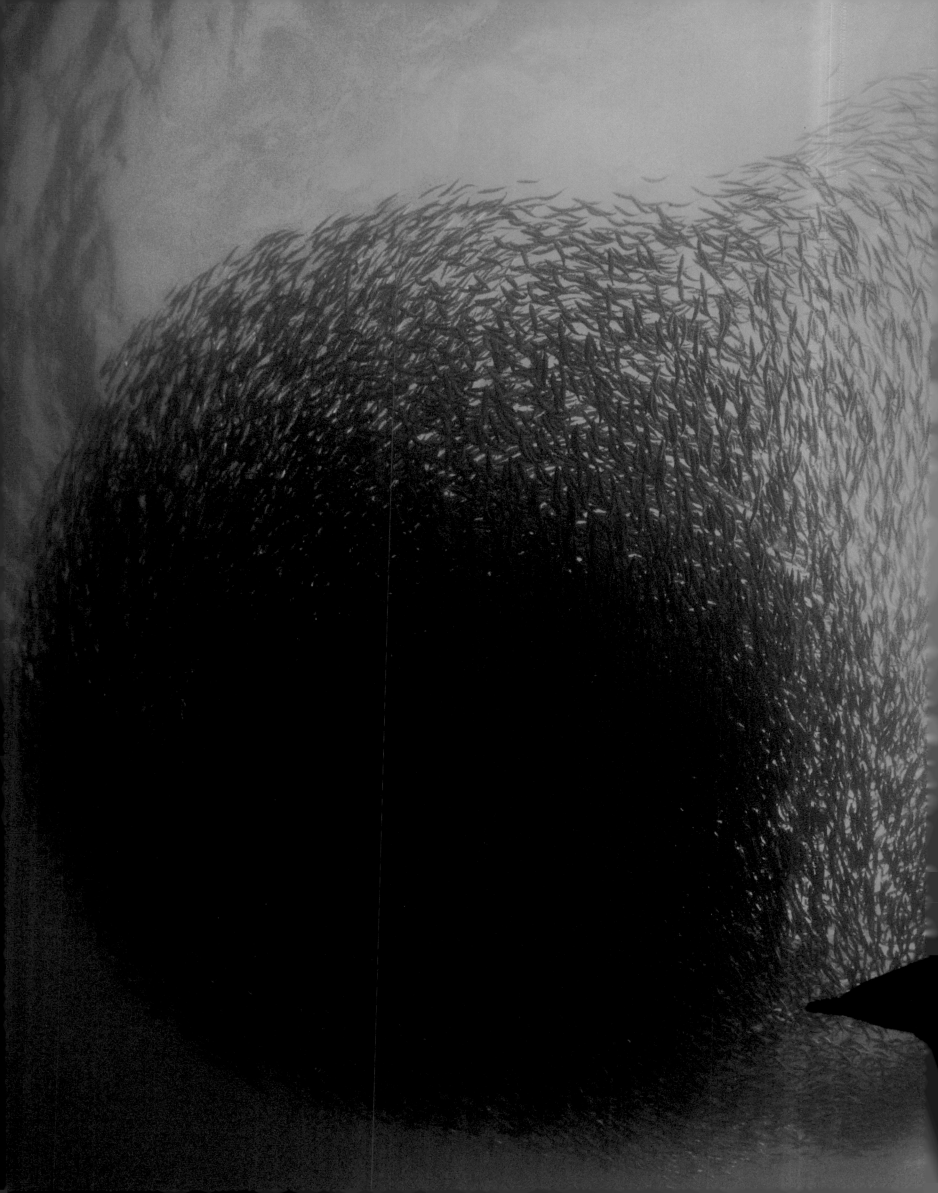

🔺 Thousands of common dolphins join together in super alliances to round up sardines and drive them up toward the surface, resulting in the formation of bait balls. Frightened sardines instinctively group together as a defense mechanism.

↟ The common dolphins work as a team to herd the sardines and feed. The bait balls can be 32 to 65 feet (10 to 20 m) in diameter and extend to a depth of 32 feet (10 m). They are relatively short-lived and intense events.

◆ Once the dolphins have rounded up the sardines into a bait ball, other predators take advantage of the fish banquet. Gannets launch aerial assaults on the sardines as they dive into the surface water to feed.

CALVES
CARING FOR THE NEXT GENERATION

CALVES

CARING FOR THE NEXT GENERATION

During the summer, killer whales (*Orcinus orca*) are often seen in waters off southern Vancouver Island, British Columbia, and northern Washington, where they gather to eat migratory salmon. Among them, an orca nicknamed Granny, the oldest female in the southern resident population of orcas that live in the Pacific Northwest, is swimming alongside her son, Ruffles. At 99 years old, Granny is the matriarch of the J pod, one of the three pods that make up the southern group. Ruffles is 59 and has always lived with his mother. The strong lifetime family bonds that exist among these orcas and the fact that individual animals never leave their social group are very unique among all mammals. The orcas feed on specific salmon runs, and over the centuries, they have developed a specialized knowledge of where and when to find their favourite fish. There is a real advantage for the younger animals to stay with their mothers and grandmothers, who possess all this knowledge and share it with the next generation.

The resident killer whales off the coast of Washington and British Columbia are dedicated mothers and grandmothers. They are not the only ones. Cetaceans provide a great deal of care to their young. They reproduce slowly, giving birth in the water to one calf at the time, in which they invest heavily. For baleen whales, the gestation period ranges between 10 and 13 months, and for toothed whales, gestation ranges from about seven months for Dall's porpoises (*Phocoenoides dalli*) to 16 months for sperm whales (*Physeter macrocephalus*) and killer whales. It takes a long time because the calf must be fully developed to be able to swim, breathe, suckle, and see straight away the moment it is born. The calf comes into the world tail first, and will be dependent on its mother for some time, often for years.

Killer whales reach reproductive age between 12 and 15 years and have a single calf every three to five years during a 25-year reproductive cycle. Other toothed whales may have shorter breaks between calves. Baleen whales typically reach puberty early, at five to seven years of age. Humpback whales (*Megaptera novaeangliae*) become sexually mature at six to eight years in the North Pacific, but do not begin to have calves until they are almost 12 years old. Grey whales (*Eschrichtius robustus*) become sexually mature between five and 11 years of age, or when they are about 40 feet (11 or 12 m) long.

When it comes to motherhood, baleen whales follow the rhythms of annual migrations, from feeding grounds in the summer to breeding areas in the winter. In the Pacific, the breeding season for humpback whales generally begins in December. Conception is followed by about 12 months of gestation during which a pregnant female will travel north and back again, timing her arrival in the breeding grounds for the birth of the calf. Similarly, when a pregnant grey whale arrives in the sheltered, warm lagoons of Baja California, Mexico in late December or early January, she is ready to give birth, if she has not done so already during migration. There are several advantages to giving birth in warm tropical waters. Calves do not have much blubber when they are born, so the warm water compensates for their lack of insulation. The salinity of the water also helps them to stay afloat. Because of the physical demands of producing, suckling, and intensively caring for a calf, especially while migrating, females usually have a rest period of about two years before having another calf.

While the breeding grounds of some cetaceans are well known such as the Mexican lagoons that grey whales use, researchers have spent years looking for places where blue whales (*Balaenoptera musculus*), the planet's largest animals,

140-141 A bottlenose dolphin calf swims near its mother near the Bonin Islands, Japan. The strongest bond among dolphins is that between mother and calf. Calves travel near their mother's dorsal fin or just ventral to her for protection during swimming.

have their babies,. In 2008, they encountered a baby blue whale in the Costa Rica Dome in the tropical Pacific Ocean and were able to establish this region as the only confirmed nursery for the blue whale.

Female cetaceans, like other mammals, produce milk, and cetacean calves nurse just as human babies do. The challenge is that newborn calves cannot hold their breath for very long, so mothers often suckle them in short bouts. As they grow, they nurse them less frequently but for longer periods. The calves grow very fast thanks to the rich milk they feed on. Whales' milk is much thicker than the milk of terrestrial mammals. It has less water, and it is extremely high in fat. Human milk is about 2 percent fat while cetacean milk is 40 to 50 percent fat. This rich drink allows cetacean calves to grow quickly and develop a thick layer of blubber that will keep them warm. On this high-calorie diet, a calf's growth rate is impressive. For example, during the seven months that a blue whale calf is nursing, it will gain about 175 pounds (80 kg) a day. It will grow from 23 to 53 feet (7 to 16 m) long and from 3 to 23 tons. Newborn grey whales are about 15 feet (4.5 m) long and weigh about 1,100 pounds (500 kg). As they drink 3 to 6 gallons (13 to 22 litres) of 53 percent fat milk every day, they double their weight and add several feet to their length by the time they are weaned, seven or eight months later. It has been estimated that their daily weight gain is close to 200 pounds (91 kg) per day, or 8 pounds (3.5 kg) per hour. The caloric demands of a growing baleen whale are so intense that their mothers will lose a quarter to a third of their body weight while nursing. Most whale mothers wean their young sometime during the first year, but some calves are nursed for longer, particularly among toothed whales. The last-born of older sperm and pilot whales have been known to suckle for 13 to 15 years.

A calf depends entirely on its mother for survival. For example, a grey whale mother will nurse the calf, teach it how to navigate the coastlines to the northern feeding grounds, and eventually show it how to feed on its own. Yet, after their first year, toothed and baleen whales lead very different lives. Once baleen whales are weaned, they have little or no further contact with their mothers and go their separate ways. On the other hand, toothed calves tend to stay with their mothers' group for a longer period of time. Among dolphins, the intimate bond between mother and calf is very strong. Calves travel near their mothers' dorsal fin or just ventral to her for protection and assistance during swimming. They swim so close to their mothers that they literally get sucked along. The movement of water around the body of the mother dolphin pulls the calf sideways towards her, and the calf is transported without moving a muscle.

Bottlenose dolphin calves stay with their mothers for two to four years, and they have a lot to learn if they are to survive. In a well-studied population of bottlenose dolphins in Monkey Mia, Shark Bay, Australia, researchers have shown that newborn dolphins spend on average more than 96 percent of their time within 30 feet (9 m) of their mothers, although the amount of time they spend near their mothers decreases as they grow older. They explore their new environment and engage in social play with other young dolphins, but continue to associate closely with their mothers until weaning. After they are weaned, females tend to stay in the same areas as their mothers while males range slightly farther than females. However, when they become adults, the home ranges of both sexes continue to overlap with that of the mother.

Bottlenose dolphin calves accompany their foraging mothers and have many opportunities for learning hunting tricks be-

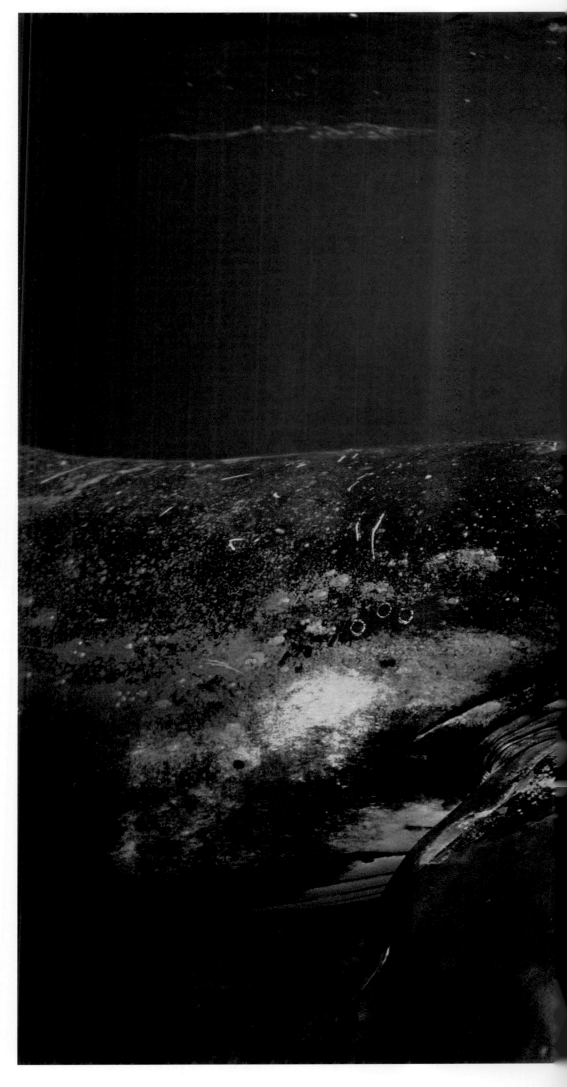

A humpback whale calf swims above its mother in French Polynesia. Among whales, the care of offspring falls to the mother. Sperm whale or dolphin groups will defend a calf, but for the more solitary baleen whales, like this humpback, the mother is the first and last line of defense against predators. ▶

♠ A humpback whale mother and calf swim close to each other in the Dominican Republic. Humpback whale calves are born at wintering grounds in tropical and subtropical regions. Newborn calves can generally be identified by their light coloration and their relatively small mouth area, compared to adult whales.

A humpback whale mother looks after her calf in the Kingdom of Tonga. After a gestation period of about a year, females give birth to a single calf. Most calves are weaned and independent from their mothers by the time they are one year old. A newborn calf may consume more than 100 gallons of milk a day. ▶

In the Pacific Ocean, a humpback whale calf stays close to its mother. The bond between a mother and her calf is very strong, and she will keep her calf close by at all times. Calves are vulnerable to many threats. Nearly 30 percent of newborn calves will not survive their first year.

♠ Closeness to its mother gives this humpback calf reassurance and protection. Within three months the calf must be large and strong enough to accompany its mother on its first migration to feeding grounds in cold polar or sub-polar waters.

◆ A humpback whale calf positions itself just above and to one side of the mother's head, back towards her pectoral fin when traveling. The calf always maintains visual contact with its mother and may take advantage of the slipstream she creates. As the calf explores its surroundings, it remains in frequent vocal contact with its mother.

A group of sperm whales swim in the Azores, Portugal. Stable, long-term groups of females form the core units of sperm whale society. These groups consist of up to about a dozen adult females accompanied by their offspring. While some of the adult females dive in search of food, others in the school mind the calves near the surface. ▶

158-159 A sperm whale mother and its calf swim close to each other in the Azores, Portugal. Females give birth only every four to six years, and the calving interval is even longer for older females. The low reproductive rate of this species allows females to invest many years of care in each calf.

160-161 A gray whale calf swims along, staying close to its mother in the breeding lagoons of Baja California, Mexico. Female gray whales calve at intervals of two or three years. The gestation period is estimated to last 12 to 13 months. At birth, gray whales are about 15 to 16 feet (4.6 m to 4.9) long and weigh about 2,000 pounds (920 kg).

162-163 A gray whale calf swims near its mother in the warm, sheltered lagoons of Baja California, Mexico. Calves are born in the winter and nurse on milk that is 53 percent fat. They become independent by seven to nine months old, prior to the fall migration. When they are born, they have very few of the barnacles and whale lice that will infest them as adults.

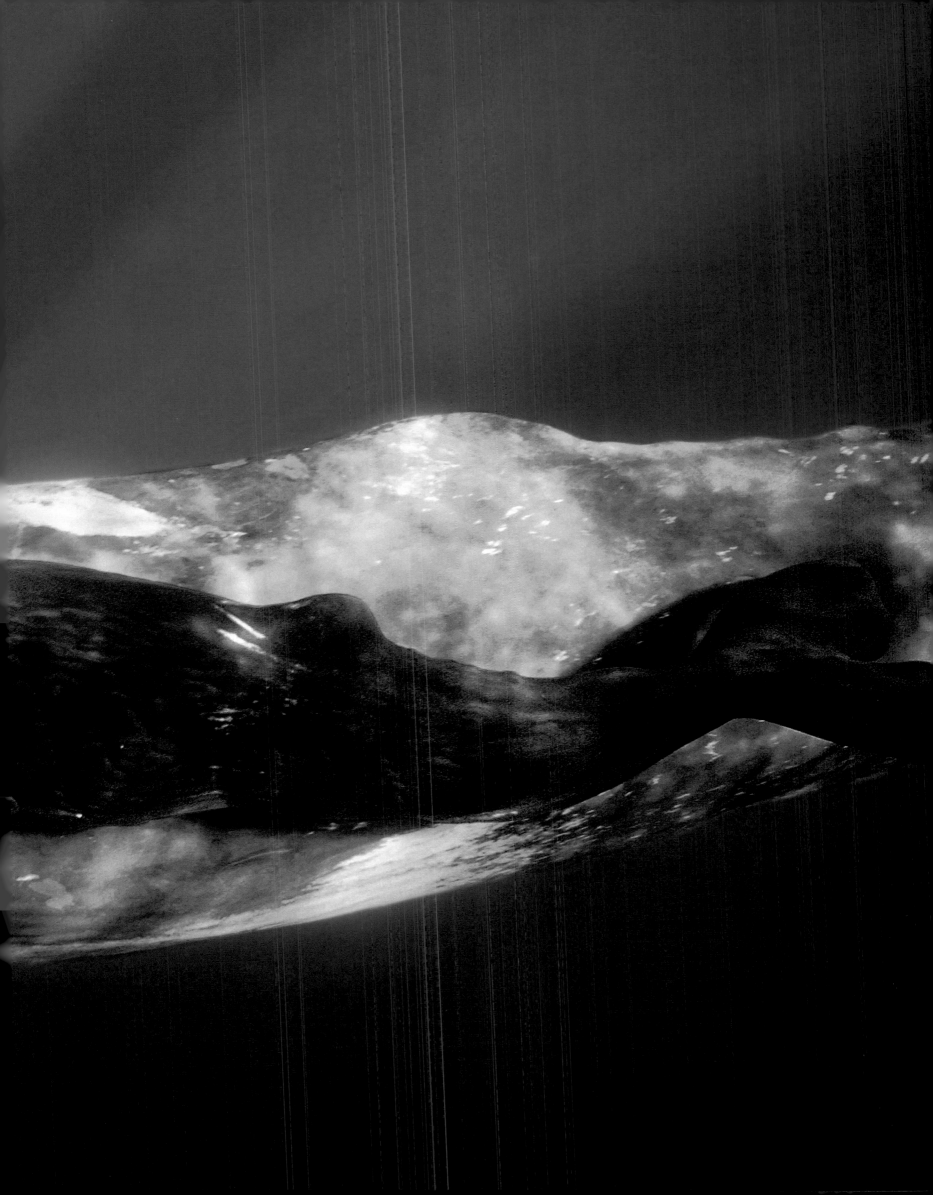

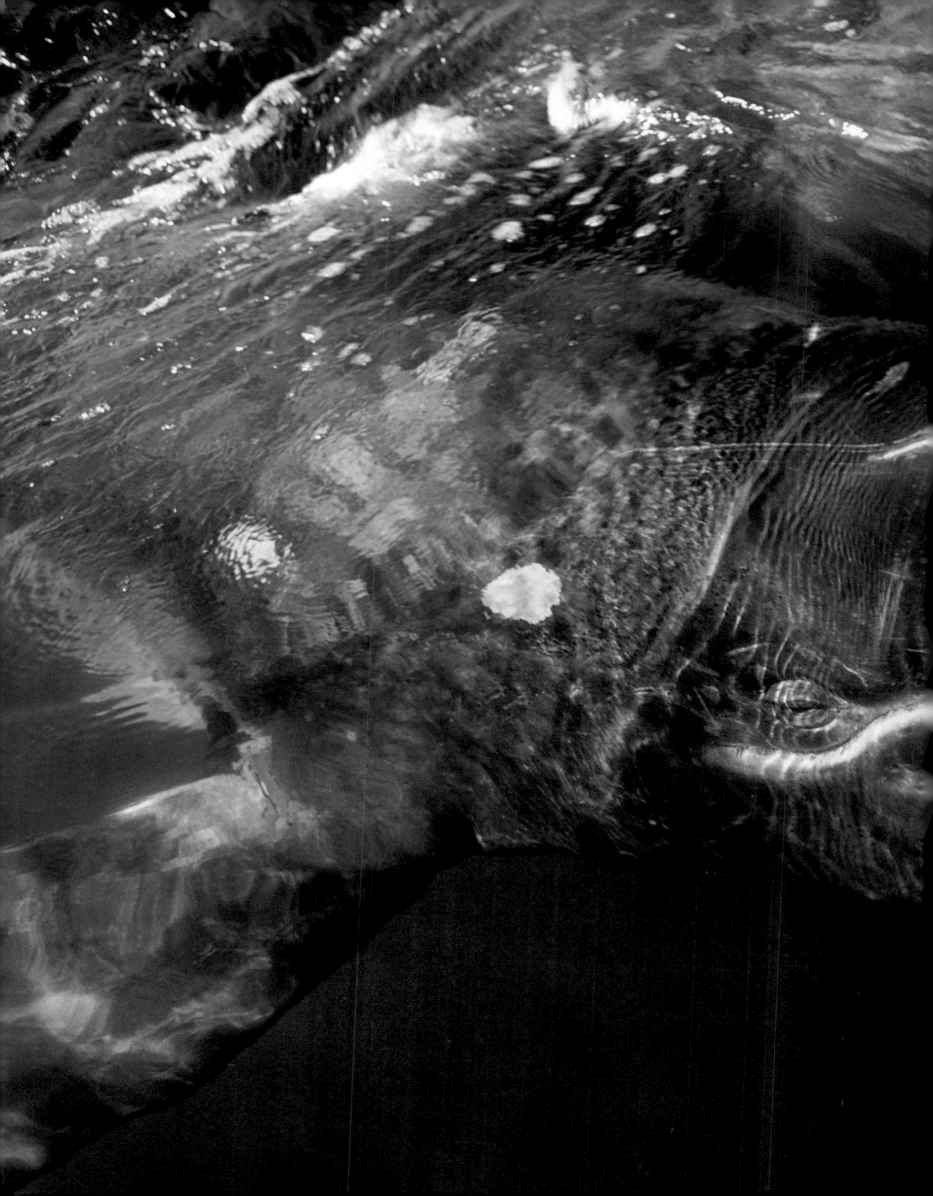

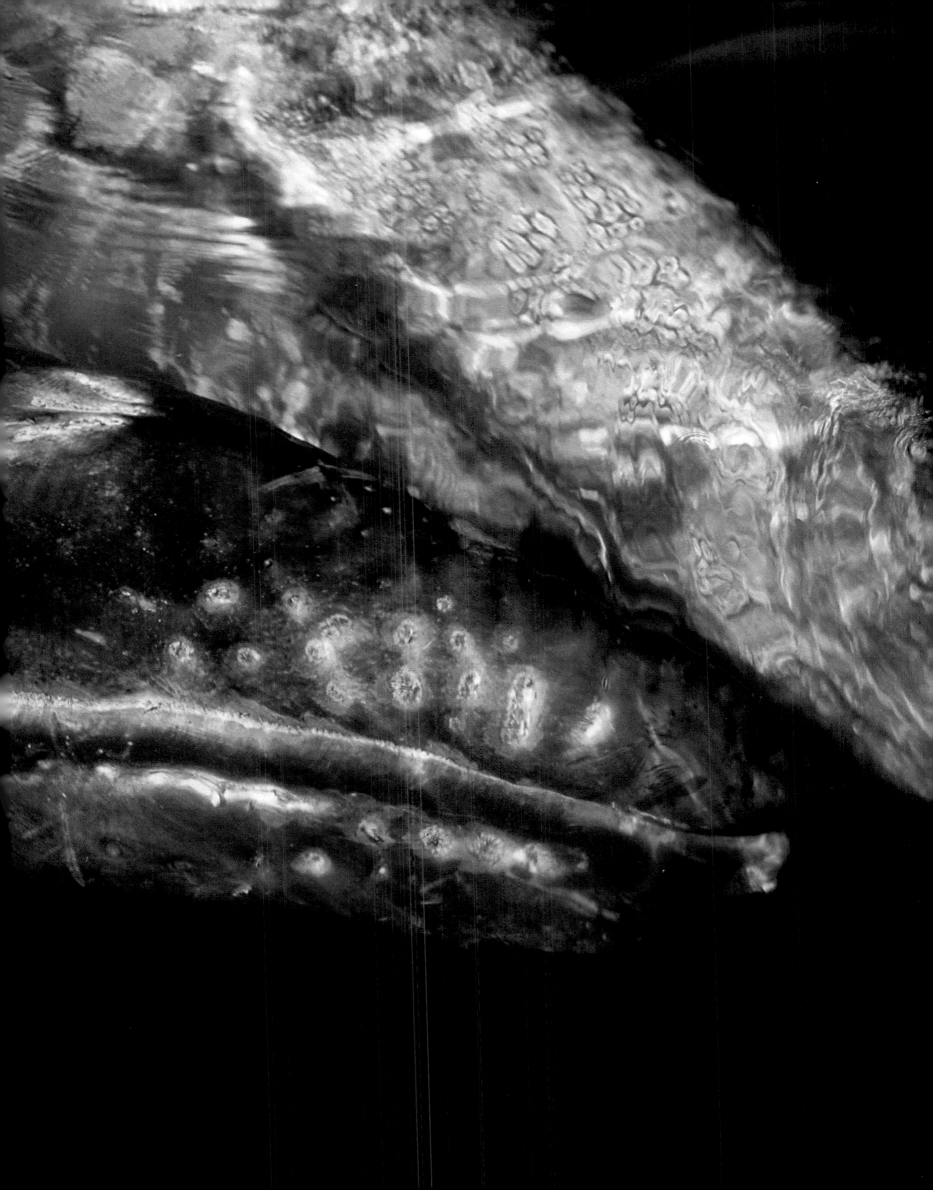

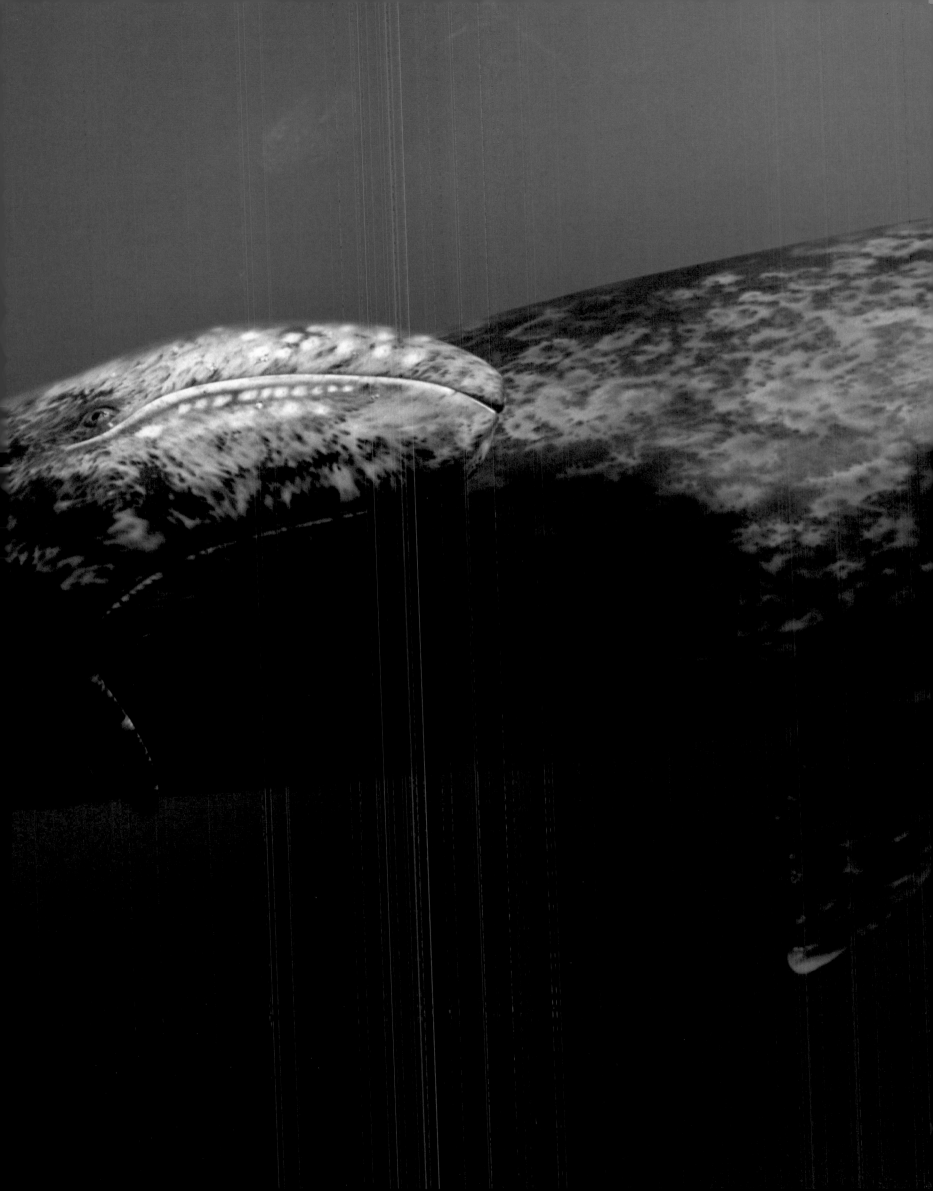

A killer whale mother and calf surface in the Ross Sea, Antarctica. Killer whales often spyhop among restricted breathing holes in icy waters. Swimming and breathing by its mother's side, an orca calf acquires critical survival skills and learns specialized hunting techniques in the harshest marine environments. ▶

A killer whale mother and calf form an intimate and lifelong bond that is the foundation of the social organization among orcas. Touch, along with hearing and sight, plays an important role in maintaining the vital, strong bond between mother and calf.

▲ Newborn killer whales nurse for at least a year and may not be fully weaned until close to two years of age. In the Pacific Northwest, gestation lasts 15 to 18 months, and the interval between calves is usually five years.

Belugas were among the first cetaceans to be brought into captivity and have been able to reproduce successfully in aquariums. This beluga whale mother and her calf reveal differences in body coloration. Calves are gray, and lighten as they age, reaching the white stage between five and 12 years of age. ▶

⬆ In the wild, the timing of reproduction for beluga whales varies by region. Gestation is estimated to last about 12 to 15 months. The calving interval averages three years.

172-173 A pantropical spotted dolphin mother surfaces with her calf in Hawaiian waters. Pantropical spotted dolphin calves are born year-round, with several seasonal peaks. The gestation period is about 11 months, and lactation lasts for at least a year, often longer than two years.

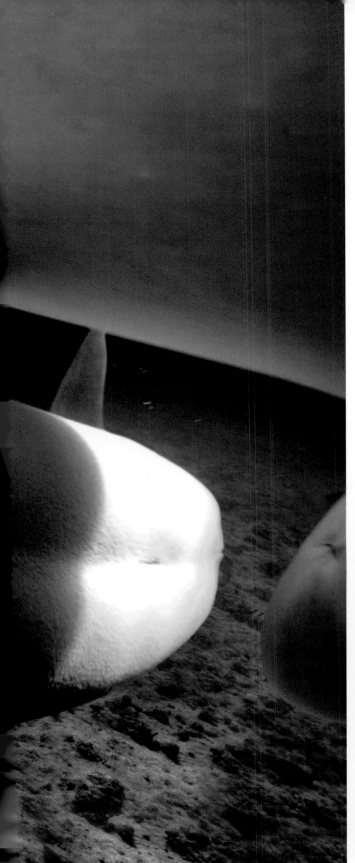

In the wild, young belugas are nursed for two years and may continue to associate with their mother for a considerable time thereafter. Belugas are highly social, occurring in close-knit pods, often of the same sex and age range. Large groups of males are observed in the summer as are smaller groups consisting of mothers and their calves.

Bottlenose dolphin mothers invest a great deal of care in their young. This mother swims close to her calf in the Bahamas and will teach her offspring many of the social skills essential for adult life in the group. Calves are often not fully weaned until 18 to 20 months of age and continue to associate with their mothers for several years. ▶

⬆ A bottlenose dolphin calf gently touches its mother in the Red Sea, Egypt. The reproductive cycle of the common bottlenose dolphin is better known than those of any other cetacean as they have been studied closely both in captivity and in the wild.

A bottlenose dolphin mother and her calf play together in the Red Sea, Egypt. Bottlenose dolphin calves can be born at any season. Gestation lasts about a year, and the average calving interval is at least three years.

A dolphin's acute hearing allows it to hunt, but it is its sense of touch that allows it to maintain bonds within a group. As these Atlantic spotted dolphins swim in the Bahamas, they spend much time touching and caressing one another with their beaks and flippers.

Members of the dolphin family display a beautiful and dramatic variation in their skin pigmentation. As this Atlantic spotted dolphin mother and her calf photographed in the Bahamas show, these markings can change with age. ▶

THE TRAVELERS OF THE OCEAN
DISTRIBUTION AND MIGRATION

THE TRAVELERS OF THE OCEAN

DISTRIBUTION AND MIGRATION

Whales, dolphins and porpoises reside in an astonishing range of aquatic habitats, from the shallow, muddy waters of the world's greatest rivers to clear tropical lagoons and ice-strewn polar waters. Some species stay in the surface layers, while others dive to the bottom of the ocean. Some remain in relatively localized areas, while others roam the world's oceans and cover great distances.

The present distribution of whales and dolphins is the result of many millions of years of climatic change, continental drift, and the evolution of the whales themselves. They have adapted to a wide range of environments, and different types of food. Many species such as the common dolphin (*Delphinus delphis*), the killer whale (*Orcinus orca*), the false killer whale (*Pseudorca crassidens*) and Risso's dolphin (*Grampus griseus*) are cosmopolitan and can be found everywhere in the world. Others are more specialized species that live in limited areas with particular climate conditions. The vaquita (*Phocoena sinus*), the world's smallest cetacean, exclusively resides in the upper Gulf of California, in Mexico. The narwhal (*Monodon monoceros*) and the beluga (*Delphinapterus leucas*) live in Arctic and subarctic waters. The rare, hard to see river dolphins exclusively live in specific rivers and are endemic to these ecosystems. They include the Amazon River dolphin (*Inia geoffrensis*) also known by its Brazilian name boto in South America, the now extinct Yangtze River dolphin (*Lipotes vexillifer*) also known as baiji in China, and the Ganges and Indus River dolphins (*Platanista gangetica gangetica* and *Platanista gangetica minor*) in India and Pakistan. Other cetaceans reside in multiple regions that are separated from each other by a geographic barrier. For example, anti-tropical distributions involve different populations of the same species separated by the equator. The Northern Right Whale

dolphin (*Lissodelphis borealis*) resides in the North Pacific, while the Southern Right Whale dolphin (*Lissodelphis peronii*), often confused with penguins because of its shape and distinctive black and white color, lives in the southern hemisphere.

Many baleen whales are great travellers and undertake long migrations every year, moving from high-latitude summer feeding grounds to low-latitude winter breeding grounds in warm waters. The same migratory behaviour occurs in both hemispheres, with a six-month difference due to the fact that when it is winter in the North it is summer in the South. Some species, such as the grey whale (*Eschrichtius robustus*) and the humpback whale (*Megaptera novaengliae*) travel thousands of miles each year. Migrating whales rarely swim non-stop. They may pause to rest or socialize, so their migration speed may vary greatly from one day to the next, but also among different species and groups. Other species of baleen whales have shorter migrations. For example, the migration of bowhead whales (*Balaena mysticetus*), found only in Arctic and subarctic waters, is seasonal and determined by retreating or advancing ice. Other baleen whales do not even migrate at all, such as some populations of Bryde's whales (*Balaenoptera edeni*) which stay in the tropics year-round.

The grey whales of the northeast Pacific are the marathon migrators, with some making round trips of more than 11,000 miles (18,000 km) per year. Their annual migration is the longest of any mammal on earth. They spend the summers in the frigid, food-rich feeding grounds in the Bering, Chukchi and Beaufort seas. When fall approaches and ice forms on the ocean surface, they begin their migration in October, heading south along the coast of North America. Their final destination is the warm lagoons of Baja California in Mexico, where they mate

180-181 A large group of long-beaked dolphins are porpoising out of the water, while moving at high speed in Plettenberg Bay, South Africa. Long-beaked dolphins are highly gregarious, and are commonly seen in herds ranging from fewer than a dozen to several thousands of animals. They sometimes associate with other species of cetaceans.

and give birth, although some females may give birth early during migration. They stay in the sheltered shallow waters of Baja California between December and March. Grey whales rarely feed on their migration and in the breeding lagoons so when they are ready to leave again by spring, they may have lost up to 25 percent of their body weight. The grey whales' migration is one of the most well known of all whales. They follow predictable routes, and usually swim very close to the coast. In the 19th century, whalers knew their travel patterns and were waiting for them every year in the bays of Baja California, almost eradicating the entire population. Today the grey whales are a major attraction for whale watchers who can observe them at close range during their migration. Their procession tends to always follow the same order. The pregnant females are first to leave the warm Mexican lagoons in February, followed by non pregnant females, mature males, and juveniles. Females with new calves are the last to leave, about a month after the rest of the group, to allow as much time as possible for the calves to grow strong enough to undertake their first migration. When the whales are again ready to leave their summer feeding grounds in the fall, their migration also follows a precise sequence. The pregnant females lead the procession south. They are followed by fertile females, mature males, and juveniles.

Like the grey whales, humpback whales have one of the longest migrations of any mammal, moving from summer feeding grounds in food-rich cool waters at high latitudes to tropical birthing and mating areas at lower latitudes. Scientists have established that some humpbacks migrating from Antarctica to Costa Rica have covered distances of more than 5,000 miles (8,000 km) one-way. They travel at an average speed of two to four miles per hour. Migration occurs in both the northern and southern hemispheres, but the humpback whales in the two hemispheres do not meet and intermingle. Most of the humpbacks migrate, although a population seems to reside in the Arabian Sea year round. In the North Pacific, humpbacks feed in waters off California, Oregon, Washington, British Columbia, the Aleutian Islands, and Kamchatka Peninsula and migrate to Hawaii, Mexico, Japan, Costa Rica, and the Philippines for mating and calving. In the North Atlantic, humpback whales feed from the Gulf of Maine through Newfoundland, Labrador, Greenland, Iceland, and Norway and migrate primarily to the West Indies, where they mate and calve. Individual whales don't always travel to the same breeding grounds, and what determines their final travel plans is still a mystery. In the North Pacific, the Hawaiian Islands are home to the largest known reproductive assembly of humpback whales in the North Pacific Ocean.

In their summer feeding grounds, the whales gorge heavily on shrimp-like crustaceans called krill and various types of small schooling fish, including herring, capelin, and sand lance. They pack on the pounds for the long journey ahead. They will not eat again for a long time, as migration routes and breeding areas offer the whales little opportunity to feed. During the fall, the parade of humpbacks leaving feeding grounds is predictable. Females with calves leave first, followed by immature whales. Next come mature males and females that are not pregnant. Females in their final stages of pregnancy are the last to leave, taking advantage of the bountiful food supply before travelling to food-poor areas in the south. Once they reach their breeding grounds, the whales mate and give birth in warm waters. After a few months in the tropics, newly pregnant females leave first, followed by immatures, adult males, and lastly, females with calves that have become strong enough to endure their first migration.

While the migration patterns of humpback and grey whales are well-known, the details of the journeys undertaken by blue whales (*Balaenoptera musculus*), the planet's largest animal, still remain a mystery to the scientists who have attempted to follow them across the oceans. For a long time, it was assumed that the blues followed the same migration pattern as humpback and grey whales. Yet the movements of the blues appear to be more complicated than that, and there seem to be no specific areas where large numbers of female blue whales gather to give birth. Instead their seasonal travels are not consistent and seem to change over time, as the blues follow krill, their favourite food. The females disperse at the end of the feeding season, using a number of different areas to mate and calve. The unpredictability in the blue whales' travel patterns may have perhaps saved them from being completely exploited to extinction by whalers. While grey whales consistently arrived in the Gulf of California every year where whalers would wait for them, the blues would change their migration routes from year to year, making it very difficult for whalers to find them. However, there is growing evidence that the blues are returning to pre-whaling feeding grounds, and scientists have suggested that they are re-establishing historical migration patterns, from the coast of California to areas off British Columbia and the Gulf of Alaska.

Many toothed whales are nomadic rather than truly migratory. Their movements are dictated more by the changing distribution of prey than by patterns of feeding and breeding. Mature male sperm whales (*Physeter macrocephalus*) are an exception, feeding on squid in cold high-latitude waters in the summer and moving to lower-latitude warmer waters in the winter, where they meet up with females who stay there year-round. Some toothed whales, such as the belugas of the Arctic, have shorter distance migrations that may vary with environmental conditions. The belugas spend the summer in bays and estuaries, and as those begin to freeze in the fall, the belugas move away and winter near the edges of pack ice or in areas of shifting, unconsolidated ice.

One of the mysteries researchers have been trying to solve for many years is why baleen whales migrate to low-latitude regions of the world which typically have little food to offer compared to colder waters. After all, it would seem more reasonable to remain in areas where food is abundant. Scientists have offered various explanations as to why whales migrate. For example, it has been suggested that whales leave polar regions when temperatures drop because they would expend more energy keeping warm than they would swimming to more temperate waters. Most breeding grounds are warmer, shallower, and more protected than summer feeding areas, which may make it easier for the newborn calves which still have thin blubber and are more vulnerable to heat loss. Of course, some whales spend their entire lives in the cool waters of the Arctic, and their calves are able to cope. It might also be that whales follow ancient travel corridors that evolved when the world's oceans and the positions of the continents were quite different. Some researchers believe that the mothers migrate to low-latitude waters to give birth because there, they can protect calves from the attacks of killer whales, which generally prefer cooler waters. For example, Eastern pacific grey whales give birth and nurse their young in the shallow lagoons of Baja California where killer whales are rarely found. Off Central California, mothers and their calves migrate within 200 to 400 meters of shore. They follow the contour of the shoreline and often swim inside islets and along kelp beds, again to protect themselves from killer whales. North Atlantic and southern right whales (*Eubalaena glacialis* and *Eubalaena australis*) also migrate to coastal, shallow-water breeding areas to defend calves from killer whale attack. Female southern right whales in Argentina spend a lot of time rearing their newborn calves in waters as shallow as five meters, and retreat to these shallow waters when killer whales approach. Migration patterns and distribution of bowhead whales may also be influenced by killer whales, with some researchers suggesting that bowheads tend to migrate close to coastal shallow waters in the fall for better protection against killer whales. All of these various hypotheses to explain migration patterns remain open to debate.

The other intriguing question about the journeys whales undertake is how they manage to navigate across vast expanses of featureless oceans, successfully arriving at their seasonal destinations that may be mere reefs or tiny islands. It is not fully understood how the whales know where they are and how they find their way, but it is thought that they may use various environmental and sensory navigational aids such as seafloor bottom contours, ocean currents, prominent visual landmarks and even the "taste" of water from rivers and bays. Some researchers maintain that whales create an "acoustic map" of their world and that they recognize acoustical markers and landmarks just as we use visual cues. The whales' ability to detect variations in the Earth's magnetic field is also believed to play a role in navigation.

Sometimes the whales do not get the navigation right, they become disoriented and crash ashore, a phenomenon known as stranding. Many species of cetaceans, including sperm whales, pilot whales, bottlenose dolphins and beaked whales strand on beaches worldwide. What causes whales and dolphins to end up on the beach is not always known. Sometimes a stranding occurs because an animal is injured, ill, or simply too old. Other strandings may result from navigation errors. Such errors could be caused by a disruption in the whales' magnetic sense, changes in the Earth's magnetic field, storms, reduced visibility, or noise pollution. Many mass whale strandings around the world have been connected to military sonar tests, in regions such as the Pacific Northwest of the United States, the U.S. Virgin Islands, the Canary Islands and Japan. Evidence of the danger caused by these systems surfaced in 2000, when whales of four different species stranded on beaches in the Bahamas. Earlier in that same area, the United States Navy had conducted tests of a new kind of sonar.

Once stranded, whales are subject to extreme stress. They can be injured in surf or on rocks. No longer supported by water, they may be crushed or suffocated by their own weight. Sand can block their blowholes or damage their eyes. The wind and the sun dry and burn their sensitive skin, and they may be attacked by predators.

As boat traffic increases in all oceans of the world, the migratory routes of whales can be severely disrupted. When whales are travelling across the ocean, they can collide with ships, resulting in serious injuries for the whales. Some may escape such encounters with broken ribs or a few internal injuries that heal on their own. Less fortunate whales may die from their injuries and eventually strand. Ship strikes are a major cause of mortality for various species of baleen whales, especially northern right whales, fin whales (*Balaenoptera physalus*), and humpback whales. Up to one third of all fin and right whale strandings have been attributed to ship strikes in some areas. Right whales are especially vulnerable to collisions with boats because of their behaviours and characteristics. They are black in colour, with no dorsal fin, making them hard to see. The whales also spend extended periods of time near the surface of the water and tend to be slow to respond to approaching vessels. Ship strikes are such an important factor in the lack of recovery of the critically endangered northern right whale that changes in shipping traffic speed and location, and placement of dedicated spotters on ships have been advocated to minimize future deaths. Along the California coast, migrating grey whales are commonly hit by ships. Blue whales are also impacted, and an analysis of two decades of blue whale strandings along the California coast from 1988 to 2007 has demonstrated that the blues are vulnerable to ship strikes during their seasonal travels in the area, particularly when they look for krill located in shipping lanes.

Shipping traffic and noise pollution are increasing worldwide and will continue to impact cetaceans unless we learn to give whales the space they need to continue their ancestral journeys across the oceans without being disturbed.

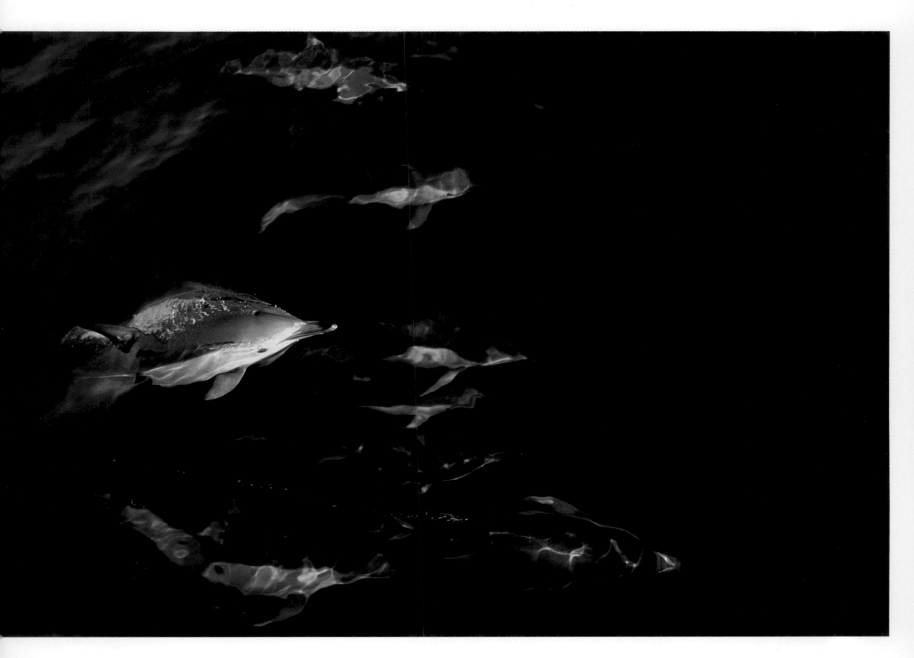

♠ Common dolphins swim in the calm waters of Golden Bay, New Zealand. Not much is known of the composition of common dolphin schools, but it is suspected that they are segregated by age and sex.

Bottlenose dolphins forage behind the surf line in Walker Bay, South Africa. Bottlenose dolphins have some of the most sophisticated hunting behaviors of any cetaceans. Their diet and hunting strategies depend largely on the habitat in which they live. ➡

188-189 Short-beaked common dolphins are porpoising in Monterey Bay, California. Porpoising is repeated leaping as a dolphin travels from one place to another. With each leap, the animal breathes, and because air offers less resistance to movement than water, porpoising is an efficient method of travel.

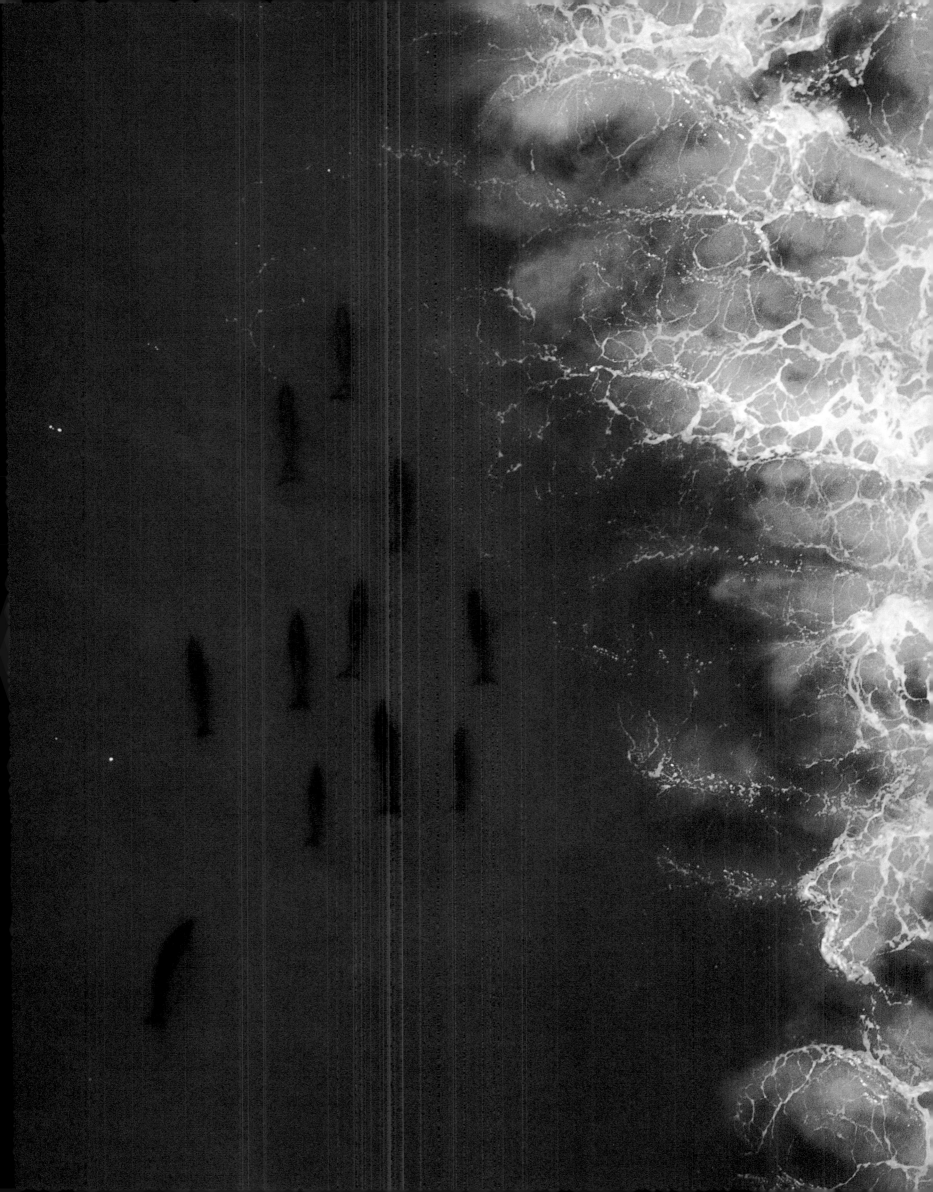

Sperm whales rest at the surface in the Caribbean between bouts of diving. There is a significant difference in migratory behavior between adult males and females. Only adult males move into high latitudes for feeding, while females and immatures stay in nursery groups in the same general area for many years. ⬧

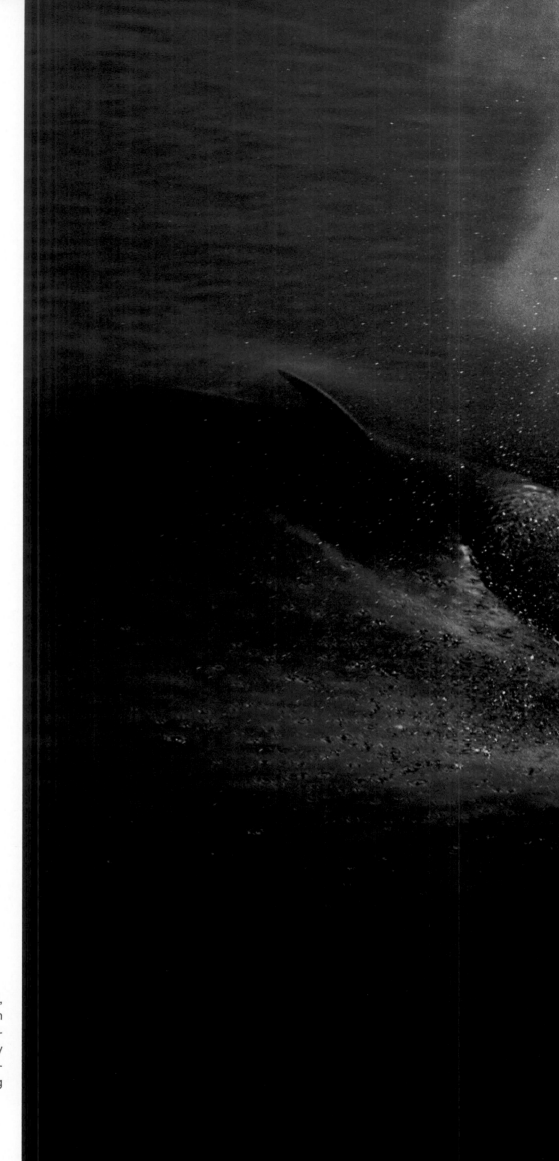

An Antarctic minke whale cruises in Lemaire Channel, Antarctica. These whales migrate to the Antarctic in the summer for feeding, and to more moderate climates in the winter for breeding. They are usually seen alone or in small groups, although larger gatherings are sometimes encountered at good feeding grounds. ▶

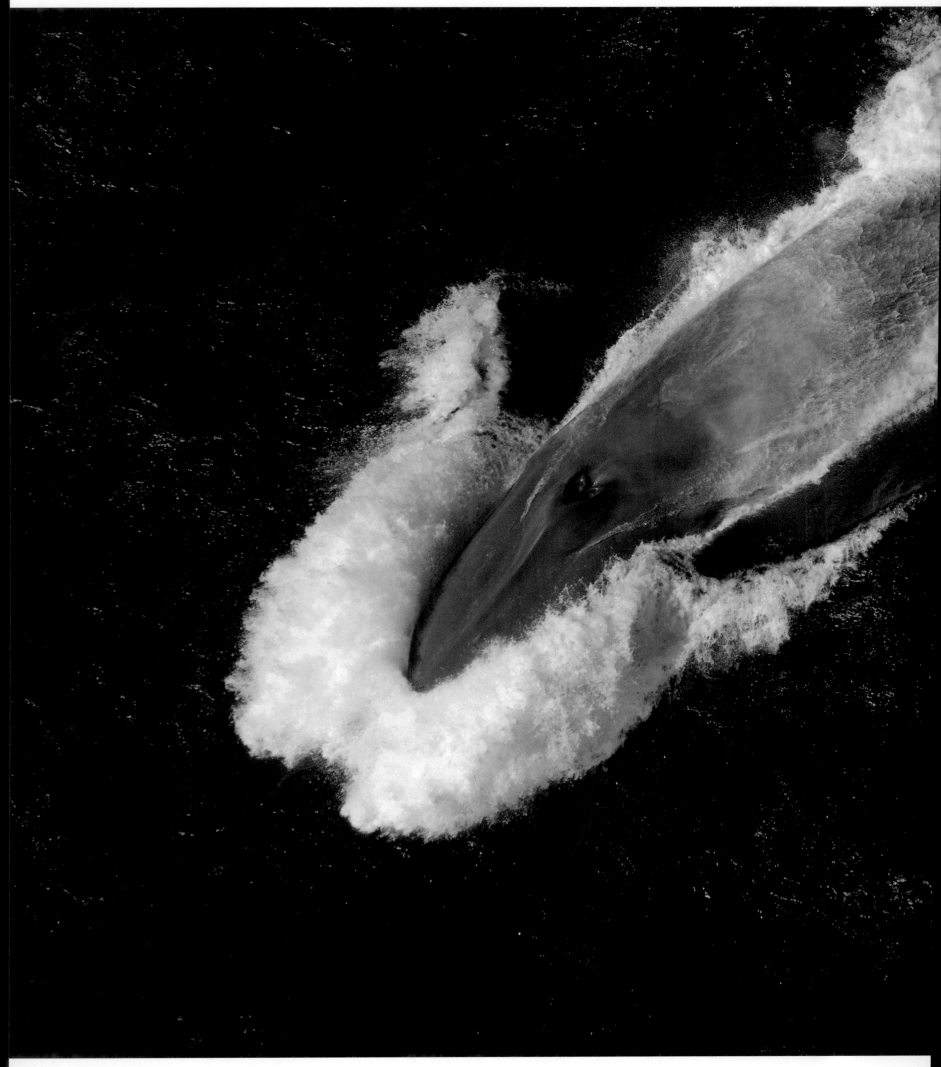

◆ A blue whale surfaces with a powerful splash in Santa Barbara Channel, California. The blue whale is the largest animal known on earth, and can reach a length of 100 feet (30.5 m). The seasonal movements of blue whales are complex. Some populations migrate long distances between low-latitude winter breeding grounds and high-latitude summer feeding grounds.

◆ A southern right whale mother and calf swim close to each other in their winter breeding grounds at Valdes Peninsula, Argentina. Females give birth to a single calf every three to five years. Calves are usually weaned and independent from their mothers toward the end of their first year.

◀ A pod of killer whales travels in the Strait of Juan de Fuca, in Washington, USA. As they travel together, pods of related killer whales often surface, blow and dive in near synchrony. Resident killer whales live in one of the most stable societies known among mammals, with individuals staying their entire lives in their natal pod.

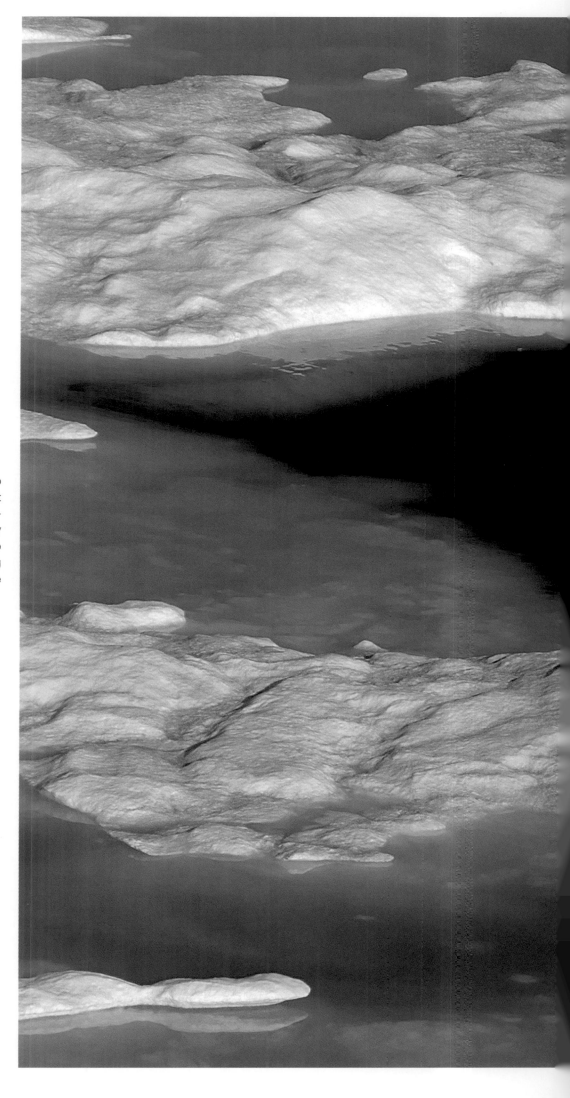

A gray whale pokes up through multi-layer ice to catch a breath of air in the Chukchi Sea, off the coast of northwest Alaska. Every year, gray whales undertake one of the longest migrations known for any mammal, about 9,000 to 12,500 miles (15,000 to 20,000 km) round trip, between winter breeding grounds in Mexico to summer feeding grounds in the Bering, Chukchi, and Beaufort seas. ▶

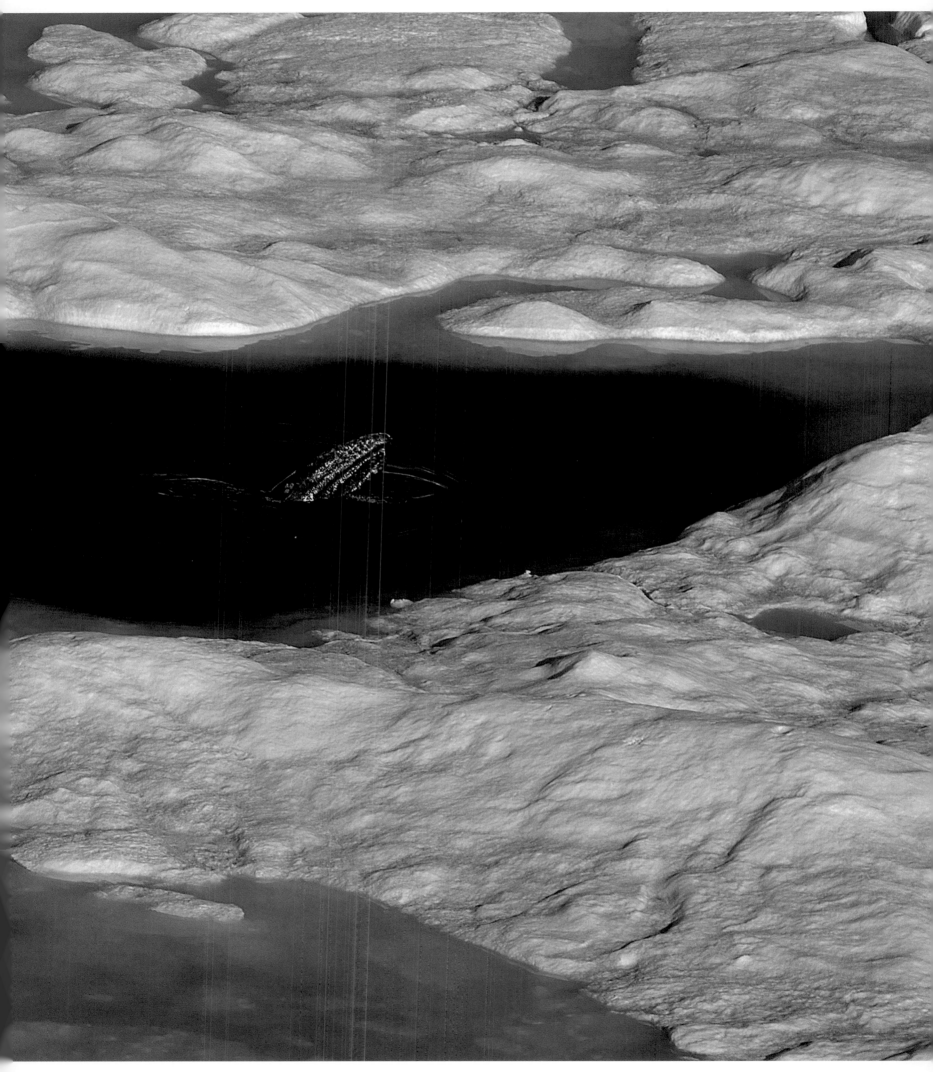

⬆ Narwhals are social animals that live in the Arctic ice. As such, they are likely to be affected by global warming more than most other species of marine mammals. They move with the receding and expanding ice edge, and may float motionless at the surface with part of the back, tusk or flipper visible.

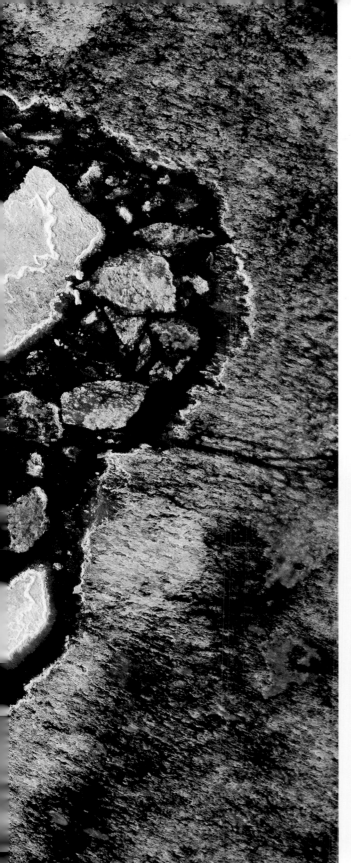

A group of male narwhals travel in waters off Baffin Island, Canada. When seen from the air, male narwhals, with their mottled coloration and unicorn tusk, are unmistakable. They usually travel and forage in groups of fewer than 20 animals, but occasionally congregate in the thousands.

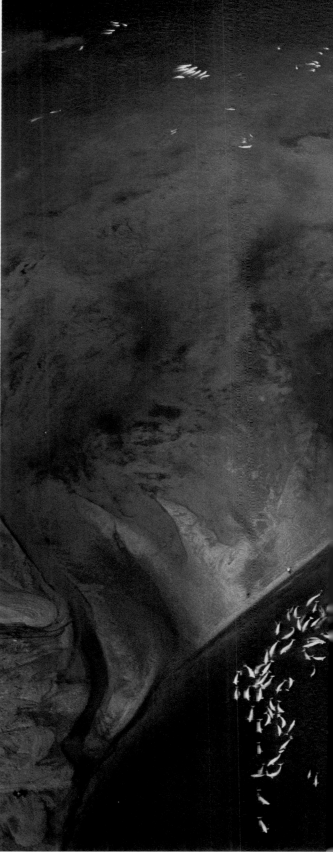

▼ Under 24 hours of sunlight, Somerset Island's shoreline in Nunavut, Canada, comes alive in the summer with thousands of beluga whales that come to breed, raise their young, and shed their skin.

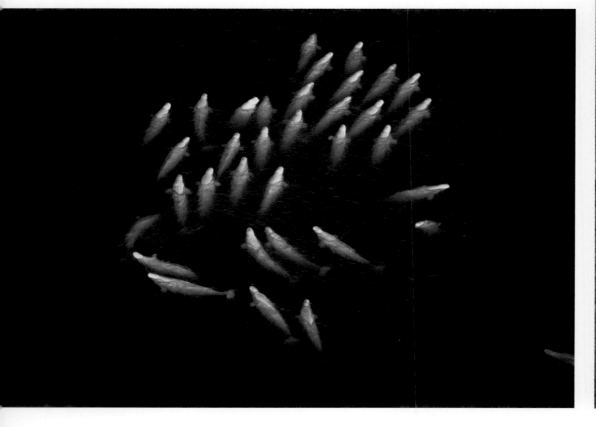

♠ Beluga whales are highly gregarious and are most often found in groups of about 15 animals. They are also seen in spectacular aggregations of thousands when they gather in shallow estuaries in the summer. They sometimes get stranded and have to wait patiently for the next high tide to float off.

LIFE IN SOCIETY
CETACEANS' SOCIAL BEHAVIORS AND COMMUNICATION

LIFE IN SOCIETY

CETACEANS' SOCIAL BEHAVIORS AND COMMUNICATION

Whales, dolphins and porpoises form complex societies and have developed many ways to live together. Some prefer solitary lives or live in small groups, while others are highly social and travel the oceans with hundreds of companions. Most toothed whales have complex social bonds, and some of their societies are matriarchal. Resident killer whales and long-finned pilot whales remain together for their entire lives. Female sperm whales live in groups of close relatives, aunts, sisters, daughters and mothers, and watch each other's calves. Some male bottlenose dolphins develop life-long friendships with other males. Other species live in fluid societies, with individuals freely coming and going. Baleen whales often live alone or in small groups, but some individuals spend more time with other whales. Humpback whales work cooperatively to get food, and their relationships can endure for many years.

Within these complex societies and social networks, cetaceans teach other communication skills, creative hunting tricks, and defense techniques against predators. These cultural traditions are passed on from generation to generation. Among whales and dolphins, vocal communication is primordial and takes on many forms, from the specialized "dialects" of orca pods to the enchanting squeaks and squeals of dolphins and the haunting songs of humpback whales.

Resident killer whales of the Pacific Northwest in North America provide one of the best examples of cetaceans with rich and complex social lives. These well-studied animals live in close social groups called "matrilines" consisting of a mother and one or more generations of her male and female descendants. Because of the long lifespan of the matriarch, some matrilines may contain four generations. The intergenerational bonds among females and their offspring are extremely strong and persist throughout the whale's life. This enduring relationship is the foundation of the resident killer whale society. The young killer whales learn from the orca matriarch and acquire vital communication, social and hunting skills. These cultural traditions are maintained and transmitted to the next generation, ensuring the survival of the whales. With the exception of some humans, killer whales are the only mammals in which both genders remain with their maternal group for life. These families associate in larger groups called pods, which share the same dialect of seven to 17 distinctive calls. Each pod of resident killer whales has a unique dialect that can be readily identified. The group's dialect is learned by each individual orca, probably by mimicking its mother as a calf. The calls are used for social communication within and between groups. Researchers believe that the need to avoid inbreeding may have driven the evolution of orca dialects, allowing the killer whales to identify who is who and ensure that they do not mate with members of their own or any closely related pod. As a result, they choose mating partners with a different "accent." Within the resident killer whale populations, pods with related dialects belong to a clan. All pods within a clan have mostly descended from a common ancestral pod through a process of growth and fragmentation in the matrilines.

Resident killer whale groups have different activities that have been classified by researchers into four categories: foraging, travelling, resting, and socializing. One particularly unusual form of socializing activity is called "beach rubbing" and involves only northern resident killer whales. In this behavior, the orcas visit specific beaches on Vancouver Island in British Columbia, Canada, where they rub their bodies on small, smooth pebbles.

While resident killer whales feed on fish, transient killer whales hunt other marine mammals such as sea lions, porpoises, harbor seals, and whales. Their diet influences how they communicate among themselves. The transients live in smaller groups and while vocalizations are important for their communication, they rely on a smaller repertoire of calls than the resident killer whales, probably because they have adapted to more silent hunting strategies and have developed other ways to share information while pursuing prey. Indeed, as they feed on marine mammals it is to their advantage to remain silent while hunting so that their prey cannot hear them.

A strong social organization is also observed in sperm whales which, like killer whales, live in long-term social units. Females, calves and juveniles of both sexes live together in stable units that persist for years. Within these groups, females share parental care for calves. While female sperm whales remain with their mother's group for life, the males tend to leave their natal unit when they reach sexual maturity and join bachelor groups. Female and male sperm whales largely live separate lives. While the females and juveniles remain in tropical and temperate waters throughout the year, mature males migrate in the summer to polar water where food is plentiful and return in the winter to socialize and mate with the females.

Sperm whales produce distinctive sound patterns unique to their social unit. These discrete calls, termed "codas" consist of a series of clicks, and are most often heard when the whales are socializing. Researchers have shown that sperm whales belonging to a particular social unit tend to associate with other units possessing similar coda repertoires. Shared codas serve to confirm group identity, maintain social bonds, and may signal affiliation to a higher-order social structure, the "vocal clan." They may also allow group members to keep track of each other when they disperse during foraging dives.

While killer whales live in the most closely knit societies on earth, many other dolphin species are gregarious, and display various types of social relationships and dynamics. Dolphin societies are complex, differ from species to species, and even vary among various populations of the same species. Some factors influence group size, such as prey type, distribution, and predator pressure. Bottlenose dolphin groups typically average 10 to 25 individuals, but membership in a group will change over time. Some dolphin societies have been described as having a "fission-fusion" dynamic, similar to primates. In this model, dolphins spend a lot of time in small groups travelling, foraging, and playing. They come together to form larger groups for socializing, coordinated hunting, and other activities. When they are finished, dolphins break back into smaller groups with the same or different members as before. There are exceptions to this social organization in

206-207 A group of sperm whales interact. The social system of sperm whales has been well-studied. When searching for mates, adult male sperm whales visit various nursery groups of social adult females and their offspring. The female groups are characterized by long-term stability.

some dolphins. For example, well-studied bottlenose dolphins in Florida and Australia are known for the strong relationship between mother and calf, in which the young dolphins remain close to their mothers for several years. Other strong relationships are formed by males who develop lifelong friendships. In these small, "first-order" alliances formed between two or three males, the dolphins work together to herd females during the mating season. In Shark Bay, Western Australia, researchers have discovered that these strong, enduring, small male alliances can form temporary, "second-order" alliances with other male dolphins to increase their success while courting females. Even more complicated partnerships involving a larger number of dolphins and called "super-alliances" are also formed.

Dolphins have a rich vocal repertoire. They mainly use pulsed sounds that are short in duration, and whistles of mid- to high frequencies of longer duration. The whistles vary across species as well as within species across geographic locations, social groups, populations and individuals. Dolphins produce distinctive whistles called "signature whistles" that uniquely identify a dolphin and allow individuals to recognize one another. Through signature whistles, dolphins call each other by name. These individually distinct whistles are thought to maintain group cohesion, individual bonds, and contact among individual dolphins that are separated by distance. Because bottlenose dolphins live in a fission-fusion society and individuals choose to join or leave a group, whistles are particularly important to locate other dolphins, and coordinate group movements and hunting efforts. For example, iso-

lated group members may use a specific whistle to let their companions know that they are nearby or that they want to regroup. Bottlenose dolphin whistles have been the focus of scientific debate, with some researchers stating that dolphins have signature whistles used as unique identifiers, and others emphasizing that they also share a repertoire of whistles with others in the population. There is still much to learn about the significance of the differences detected in the whistles produced by dolphins.

In addition to whistles and various sounds in their vocal repertoire, dolphins have other ways to communicate with their peers. Touch and body language are particularly important among dolphins to strengthen social bonds, establish dominance, or engage in courtship. They stroke or pat one another with their flippers or flukes, and rub bodies together. Calves swim close to their mothers and gently rub against each other. Pairs of male dolphins also engage in synchronous behavior, often surfacing to breathe, leaping, diving, and traveling in perfect unison. Research suggests that the males are using synchronous behavior to demonstrate their bond and their ability to work together as a strong team toward a common goal.

Baleen whales also vocalize to communicate with each other. Hearing is their most important sense, and they very much depend on sound, which travels faster in water than in air, to communicate. Different species across the world have different vocal repertoires, and researchers are just beginning to understand the rich acoustic world of the whales. For example, bowhead whales have developed sophisticated songs that are used to attract mates. They change their songs from year to year and never repeat songs from previous years.

On their breeding grounds, male humpback whales sing long, complex songs for hours at a time and that are so loud they can sometimes be heard above the water's surface. A humpback song generally lasts between five and 20 minutes, and is an organized sequence of sounds. The song is composed of a series of discrete notes or units, and a series of units constitutes a phrase. Phrases may contain repeated sounds, and a consecutive group of phrases makes up a theme. The song then shifts to a different set of units and phrases repeated in a new theme, and so on. The entire song is a series of five to seven different themes. A sequence of songs separated by brief pauses constitutes a song session. The whale's song constantly evolves over time, and as the breeding season progresses new themes may be introduced or old ones may be changed, so that by the end of the breeding season, the song can be quite different from the song heard at the beginning. Each singer learns from other humpback whales, and changes its song to keep in tune with other singers. All male humpback whales in a given breeding area perform the same song.

Researchers have long wondered about the function of the humpback song, and there is still debate on why these songs are performed. Male humpback whales sing mostly during the breeding season, and may do so for a variety of reasons: to attract females, signal their presence to other males and drive them away or on the contrary interact with them, and assess the location and distance at which potential rivals may be.

Blue whales have the deepest voices of any animal, and their mighty vocalizations carry for thousands of miles underwater, allowing them to communicate across vast oceans. Scientific knowledge about the blue whale's acoustic world is still sketchy, but it is assumed that males sing songs across the vast expanses of the ocean to attract potential mates and warn away other males. Research suggests that the sound level of these songs has been steadily declining for the past few decades. Indeed, studies of blue whale song data from around the world show that while the basic style of singing remains the same, the animals are shifting the pitch, or frequency, of the songs down over time. Researchers have examined a list of possible explanations for this drop in frequency. from climate change to a rise in human-produced ocean noise. They believe the change may be explained by the increase of blue whale numbers following bans on commercial whaling activities. Blue whales are widely dispersed during the breeding season and it is likely that songs are used to locate potential females for mating as well as male competitors. At the peak of commercial whaling, as blue whale numbers plummeted, it may have been advantageous for males to sing higher frequency songs in order to maximize their transmission distance and their ability to find females which might have been located a long way away. In other words, the blues needed to shout to make themselves heard. Now that blue whales are recovering and increasing in numbers, the closest females are not so far away anymore, and

◀ Sperm whales float upside down in the Azores, Portugal. When socializing, sperm whales use vocalizations termed "codas" that are distinct to groups of sperm whales and may act as acoustic signatures.

◆ Sperm whales have a highly complex social structure. The most common social group is composed of adult females, sub-adults, and calves of both sexes, located in low latitudes. Mature males spend most of their times at high latitudes, occasionally travelling to lower latitudes to mate.

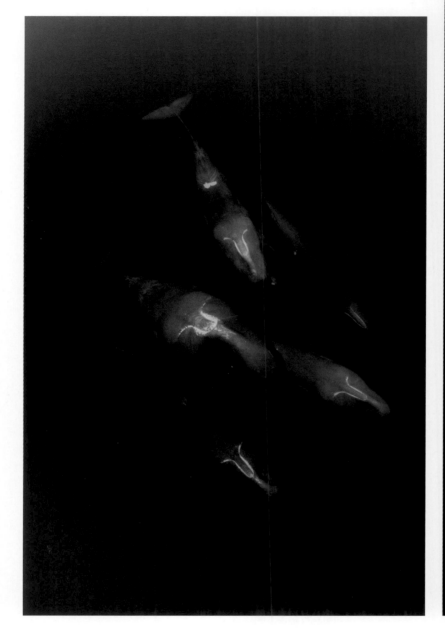

⬆ Thanks to the matrilineal social organization of the sperm whale, female adults are able to share care of the young. Sperm whales make long and deep dives to forage for squid. Calves are unable to dive deep to forage with their mothers, so other female adults watch calves at the surface while the mother goes on a foraging dive.

⬆ Three female sperm whales entwine in a ritual whose function remains unknown to us. Sperm whales plunge vertically to feed in the ocean. They are deep and long divers and can reach depths of up to 3,300 feet (1,000 m) for over one hour. They often hold their flukes high before a long dive.

The Azores Archipelago, Portugal, is a peaceful haven for sperm whale groups that spend each summer there. Females accompanied by their young, are often seen in this area. When they are resting at the surface, they occasionally allow themselves to be observed at a close distance. ➡

↟ Humpback whale mothers with calves are often joined by a male escort whale on breeding grounds in Hawaii. Once chosen by a female, a male humpback must defend his position against challengers, all seeking to become the female's main escort. Aggression among male humpbacks is often witnessed.

When a humpback whale mother and calf are joined by a large number of other whales on breeding grounds in Hawaii, the males can display aggressive behaviors, striking each other with their heads and flukes, in attempts to displace each other, remain with the mother, and perhaps gain the opportunity to mate with her. ➤

◆ A female humpback whale gently glides over a male humpback whale in Hawaii. On breeding grounds, male humpbacks sing songs for hours. While the exact function of the song is not known, it is possible that it may play a role in attracting females.

♠ Courting a humpback whale mother with calf, a humpback male escort releases a massive stream of bubbles out of its blowhole. He issues a clear warning to rivals that he will fight for his position.

♠ Male southern right whales court a female in shallow waters in South Africa. Right whales are commonly found alone or in small groups of one to three animals, but they may form groups of up to 30 whales for social and courtship behaviors.

⬆ Active groups, clearly associated with sexual behavior, of several male southern right whales and one female often form at the ocean surface, in the shallow waters off South Africa. Females will often mate with more than one male in succession.

A group of Atlantic spotted dolphins are foraging in the Bahamas. Small to moderate-sized groups, generally of 50 animals, are characteristic of the Atlantic spotted dolphins. Coastal groups typically consist of 5 to 15 animals. They are mostly shallow divers. ▶

⬆ A bottlenose dolphin plays on a sandy sea bottom. Bottlenose dolphins prey on a variety of species, depending on the habitat. Coastal animals tend to feed on fish and invertebrates that live on or near the bottom, while offshore animals eat pelagic fish and squid.

A bottlenose dolphin echolocates to find small fish buried in the sand. Bottlenose dolphins use a range of techniques to catch prey. They hunt individually and cooperatively. Some of their techniques include fish whacking, driving schooling fish onto mudflats, and partially beaching themselves to collect the fish.

⬆ A group of Atlantic spotted dolphins swim in the Bahamas. Dolphins in the Bahamas have been observed to capture fish hiding in the soft, sandy bottom by sticking their beaks into the sand. They prey on small fish, cephalopods, and benthic invertebrates.

Atlantic spotted dolphins have a fluid group structure. Like that of bottlenose and other small dolphins, groups are often segregated by age and sex. One population of Atlantic spotted dolphins in the Bahamas has been studied in great detail since the 1970s, but the species is less well known elsewhere in the Atlantic. ➡

232-233 A young Atlantic spotted dolphin is mating with an older female in the clear, warm waters off the Bahamas. Not much is known about reproduction in Atlantic spotted dolphins. Females nurse their calves for more than three years, and sometimes for as long as five.

WHALE WATCHING
WHALES AND PEOPLE

WHALE WATCHING

WHALES AND PEOPLE

A humpback calf practices breaching many times near its mother. A pod of killer whales surrounds a group of kayakers. A friendly grey whale lets people touch its back. Hundreds of spinner dolphins bow ride with a fast-moving boat. To see whales, dolphins and porpoises in their natural environment is a unique, emotional, and inspiring experience, and one that underlines the importance of protecting these magnificent creatures. People's attitudes towards whales have changed, and many across the world enjoy watching them, appreciating their beauty, intelligence, and remarkable behaviors rather than hunting them. Whale watching is also a powerful way to learn about their complex behaviors, social organization and habitat. There are many places in the world where it is possible to observe whales, dolphins and porpoises, and whale-watching should be done gently, patiently and responsibly, with the welfare of the animals always coming first.

Whale watching is an increasingly popular activity around the world, and can be done from land or on water. Many operators offer whale watching trips, and it is important to select one that behaves responsibly and follows guidelines to watch cetaceans without disturbing them. Different rules and regulations apply in different places, and it is the responsibility of whale watchers and boat operators to know what they are and follow them. Whale watching regulators are now restricting the number of operators that can view cetaceans at a given time, limiting watching time, and defining sanctuaries in which cetaceans cannot be approached. If you come in contact with operators who break the rules and put the whales at risk, let the relevant authorities know.

Whale watching is an "eyes on, hands off" activity, and we have a responsibility to cause as little disturbance as possible while watching cetaceans. Whales, dolphins and porpoises should be treated with respect. They should never been touched or fed. It is particularly important not to restrict the free movement of animals while they are being observed. Whales and dolphins are often curious about people, but we have to remember that we are uninvited guests in their world, and we should always let them determine their own path and decide whether they want to approach us or not. Vessels should never chase animals, separate individuals from a group, surround them or confine them into a space where they have no escape route. Whale watch operators should maneuver their boats carefully, slowly, and not too close, and should leave before the whales show signs of distress. The prime time to see many cetaceans is when there are in breeding grounds. At such times the whales are particularly sensitive to disturbances. Intrusive whale watching can create stress between mother and calf, and even separate them. Noise from vessels can disturb normal hunting and diving behaviors. Inappropriate whale watching can injure or kill whales through collision or raking from propeller blades, or lead them to abandon their preferred feeding or breeding grounds, threatening the lives of their present and future offspring. It is best to stay quiet while observing cetaceans. Prevent trash from entering the water; it is a hazard to cetaceans and the health of oceans.

Reputable whale watching operators follow rules, put the welfare of cetaceans first, and have a commitment to protecting the whales and the marine environment. When planning a whale watching trip, find out which local operators are recommended by wildlife or whale conservation organizations, how long they have been operating, and whether they have a good safety record. Other factors to consider when choosing a responsible operator is whether they have knowledgeable naturalists onboard, if they have good relationships with scientists and conservationists, what their success rate is at finding whales, and whether they have specialized equipment onboard such as hydrophones to let you listen to the whales. Look for operators that donate a portion of their profits to the whales, in terms of education and conservation efforts.

Encountering whales, dolphins and porpoises in the wild is a thrilling experience, but the animals can sometimes be difficult to spot, and it can be even more challenging to identify the species. When joining a whale watching trip, it is good practice to scan the horizon with binoculars and look everywhere, in front of the boat, behind, and on both sides. Patience is critical, as even in areas with concentrated cetacean populations, it can take a while to track them down. Often the first signal that a whale is in the vicinity is to see and hear its blow. Sometimes the presence of hovering birds can indicate the presence of a whale in the area, particularly if they are feeding.

Whales, dolphins and porpoises have a variety of characteristics that can help identify them. With a large whale the first clue is often its blow or spout. For example, the sperm whale's blow is angled forward and to the left, which makes it easily distinguishable from other whales. Right whales produce wide, V-shaped blows whereas fin whales have tall

blows, shaped like an inverted cone. However in most small whales, dolphins, and porpoises, the blow is low, brief, and barely visible.

Other identifying features include the body shape, size and color, head characteristics, and whether the animal has a beak or not. The Irrawaddy dolphin, for instance, has a rounded head without an obvious beak, whereas the spinner dolphin has a very long, narrow beak. Some cetaceans have striking body colors such as the white beluga or the pink Indo-Pacific humpbacked dolphin. Commerson's dolphins are strikingly black and white, while Risso's dolphins are usually covered in white scratches and scars. It can be difficult to estimate the size of an animal unless there is a reference feature, such as the length of a boat. However deciding if an animal is small (less than 10 feet [3 m]), medium (10-30 feet [3 to 9 m]), or large (more than 30 feet [9 m]) is a quick way of narrowing the range of possibilities. The animal's overall body shape, such as whether it is bulky or sleek, can be a useful clue, although many cetaceans do not reveal enough of themselves to give a good impression. Getting a clear view of the animal's head is a good way to recognize a species, and some cetaceans have unusual features. For example, the beluga has a head unlike that of any other cetacean, with a white bulging melon and no beak whereas right whales have callosities covering their heads. The presence of a tusk in the male narwhal makes this species easy to identify.

Many cetaceans have a dorsal fin, and its shape, size, and position varies greatly among species. Some fins are tall and triangular, others are rounded, and a few are no more than a hump. Some have broad bases, others have narrow bases, some are curved, while others are upright. For example, killer whales have a tall dorsal fin, particularly males. As well, the size, color, markings, position and shape of the flippers can help identify a species. For example, the flippers of the humpback whale are extremely long, up to a third of its body. Killer whales have unusually broad and rounded flippers.

The dive sequence, or the manner in which a cetacean breaks the surface to breathe, and then dives again can be quite distinctive for a given species. Whether an animal is simply travelling from one place to another or diving for food changes the nature of its dive sequence. At the start of a dive, some animals may raise their flukes high into the air while others do not, providing a distinguishing feature. For example, humpback, blue and sperm whales frequently lift their flukes before they dive. They leave a "flukeprint" at the surface – a circular swirl looking like a patch of oil – made by the turbulence from the movement of the flukes. The shape and color of the flukes, as well as markings can vary greatly between species.

The number of animals that are seen travelling, socializing or feeding together is also a useful indicator of the species encountered. Some species such as bowhead whales tend to live alone or in small groups while others, such as pilot whales, are highly social and live in large groups.

Whales, dolphins and porpoises are active animals, and some of their impressive, acrobatic, and energetic displays take place in full view on the surface of the water. They slap the water with their flippers, fins, or tails, ride in the bow

waves of boats, lift their head above the surface, and even leap high into the air and land back in the water with a tremendous splash. There is still much to understand about the meaning of many of these displays, and they are always fascinating to watch.

There are plenty of behaviors to see, hear, and interpret on a whale watching trip, and each of these behaviors has a specific term. "Breaching" occurs when a whale launches itself into the air head first, and falls back into the water with a splash. Among the large whales, humpback and right whales breach much more often than other species. Smaller cetaceans leap out of the water in a graceful arc. Spinner dolphins not only leap, but spin at the same time. "Flipper-slapping" happens when cetaceans lie on their sides or backs and slap one or both of their flippers onto the surface with a resounding splash. "Lobtailing" is an impressive display especially in large whales, involving the forceful slapping of the flukes against the surface of the water. "Spyhopping" describes a behavior in which whales and dolphins poke their heads above the surface of the water, apparently to have a look around. "Logging" refers to a form of rest behavior in which groups of whales float motionless at the surface together, usually all facing in the same direction. "Porpoising" is repeated leaping as a cetacean travels from one place to another. When travelling at high speed, many dolphins and porpoises literally leave the water each time they take a breath. Because air offers less resistance to movement than water, porpoising can be a highly efficient method of travel and helps conserve energy. In "bow-riding," dolphins, porpoises and even some whales ride the bow waves of ships, jostling for the best position where they can be pushed along in the water by the force of the wave. Certain dolphins even ride the bow waves of large whales in exactly the same way. Similarly, cetaceans can be seen "wake-riding," swimming, twisting, and turning in the wake of a boat.

It can also be very spectacular to watch cetaceans feed at sea. Rorquals gulp feed, and it is a remarkable spectacle to watch their large mouths open in front of a boat to feed on krill. Observing killer whales attack sea lions or other marine mammals is a breathtaking and dramatic experience.

It is possible to see whales, dolphins and porpoises at all latitudes. They are found near the poles, at the Equator, in rivers, along coastlines and in the open ocean. Some whales such as grey and humpback whales migrate near or along coastlines in a predictable manner year after year and all it takes is to be there at the right time. Some species have a very restricted range. For example, Hector's dolphins are only found in New Zealand.

There are many choices when it comes to deciding which cetaceans to watch and how to watch them. You can fly over Kaikoura, New Zealand to search for sperm whales, or kayak with killer whales on Vancouver Island, British Columbia, Canada. In Monkey Mia, Australia you can stand in shallow water with bottlenose dolphins, and off the Dominican Republic you can snorkel in the water while humpback whales rise around you. The range of opportunities to watch whales, dolphins and porpoises is wide and includes watching from the shore, from a boat, from the air or in the water. Boat tours run from half-day excursions to several-week ex-

peditions. You can work as a volunteer alongside scientists who monitor local populations of whales and dolphins; you can join a boat trip for only a few hours, or be on a longer whale watching trip, listening to the narration provided by cetacean experts. Commercial whale watching trips increasingly chronicle their daily observations in a systematic fashion, recording the location of the encounter, documenting behavior, and seeking to identify the species or even the precise individuals involved. Detailed photo identification catalogs exist for humpback whales and killer whales, and by taking photographs, you can help build knowledge of cetaceans. You can also report your sightings to cetacean networks that aim to learn more about cetacean abundance and distribution.

Many species tend to be plentiful only in particular areas, and they may be present only at certain times of the year. It is important to plan ahead so you are in the right place at the right time, and with the right operator. The number and types of species sighted in a particular location can vary significantly from season to season. Weather conditions, food distribution and other factors can influence the movement of cetaceans in a given area. While there are certain hot spots where sightings are relatively predictable, whales and dolphins do not follow any rules. If you are keen on seeing a particular species, it is best to spend several days in a given location and join multiple whale watching trips to optimize your chances. Every whale watching trip is different, and not knowing in advance what will happen makes it even more rewarding and exciting when whales and dolphins are encountered.

1 • Husavik, Iceland
2 • Western Isles, Scotland, UK
3 • Azores, Portugal
4 • Hermanus, South Africa
5 • Bonin Islands, Japan
6 • Tañon Strait, Philippines
7 • Monkey Mia, Western Australia
8 • Hervey Bay, Queensland, Australia
9 • Kaikoura, New Zealand
10 • Hawaii, USA
11 • Glacier Bay, Alaska, USA
12 • Vancouver Island, British Columbia, Canada
13 • Monterey Bay, California, USA
14 • Baja California, Mexico
15 • Peninsula Valdés, Argentina
16 • Antarctic Peninsula
17 • Caribbean
18 • Bar Harbor, Maine, USA
19 • Quebec, Canada
20 • Nunavut, Canada

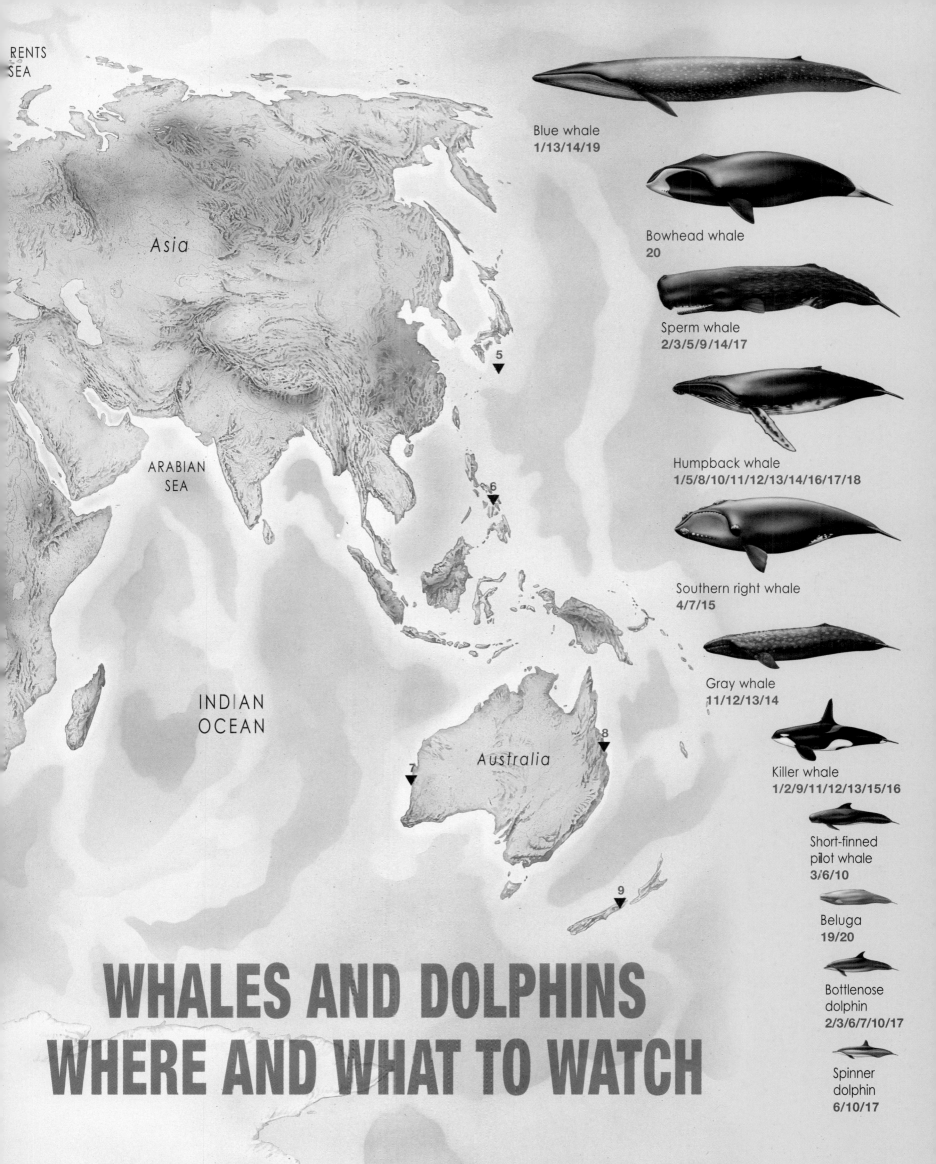

RENTS
SEA

Asia

ARABIAN
SEA

INDIAN
OCEAN

Australia

Blue whale
1/13/14/19

Bowhead whale
20

Sperm whale
2/3/5/9/14/17

Humpback whale
1/5/8/10/11/12/13/14/16/17/18

Southern right whale
4/7/15

Gray whale
11/12/13/14

Killer whale
1/2/9/11/12/13/15/16

Short-finned
pilot whale
3/6/10

Beluga
19/20

Bottlenose
dolphin
2/3/6/7/10/17

Spinner
dolphin
6/10/17

WHALES AND DOLPHINS
WHERE AND WHAT TO WATCH

Mysticeti
FAMILY BALAENIDAE

Southern right whale and
Northern right whale
(*Eubalaena australis/glacialis*)

- MAXIMUM LENGTH: 56 ft (17 m)
- MAXIMUM WEIGHT: 200,000 lbs (90,000 kg)
- DURATION OF THE IMMERSION: 10 to 20 minutes
- DEPTH OF THE IMMERSION: up to 603 ft (184 m)
- DORSAL FIN: no dorsal fin
- FLUKES AND FLIPPERS: wide, paddle-shaped flippers, up to 5.5 ft (1.7 m) long; broad, triangular flukes with smooth margins
- HEAD: large head that can be one-fourth to one-third of body length; strongly arched mouth line; head covered with callosities; right whale individuals can be identified by the patterns of scars and callosities on the head and back
- COLOR: black with irregular white patches on underside
- BLOW: distinctive short, V-shaped blow

WHALE WATCHING

- *WHEN TO GO: June to November (Bay of Fundy); April to October (Lubec); July to September (Hermanus); July to November (Peninsula Valdés); June to September (Warrnambool)*
- *WHERE TO GO: Northern right whales: Bay of Fundy, New Brunswick, Canada; Lubec, Maine, USA;*
  Southern right whales: Hermanus, South Africa; Peninsula Valdés, Patagonia, Argentina; Warrnambool, South Australia
- *SURFACE BEHAVIOUR: inquisitive and approachable; aerially active, fluke-slapping and breaching; raise their flukes before a dive; southern right whales have been observed "sailing" by catching the wind with their raised flukes*

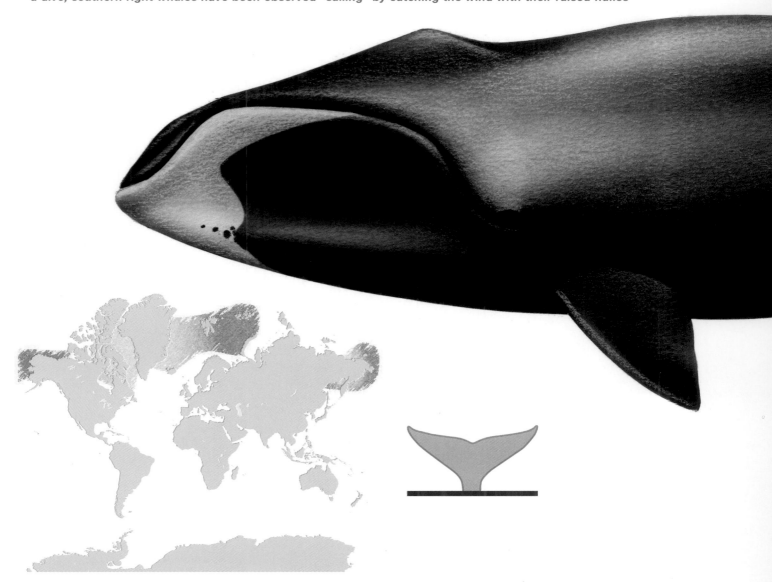

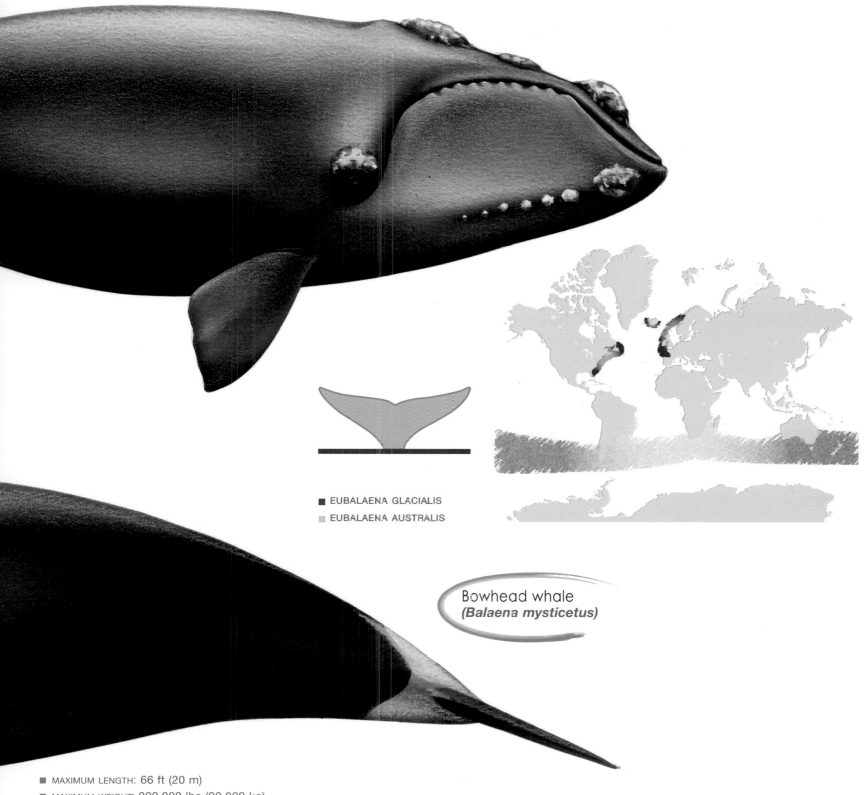

■ EUBALAENA GLACIALIS
■ EUBALAENA AUSTRALIS

Bowhead whale
(Balaena mysticetus)

■ MAXIMUM LENGTH: 66 ft (20 m)
■ MAXIMUM WEIGHT: 200,000 lbs (90,000 kg)
■ DURATION OF THE IMMERSION: from 20 minutes to an hour
■ DEPTH OF THE IMMERSION: up to 656 ft (200 m)
■ DORSAL FIN: no dorsal fin
■ FLUKES AND FLIPPERS: broad triangular flippers; very wide flukes, tapered toward the tips, with smooth contours
■ HEAD: large head; irregular white patch on chin with black spots; strongly arched mouth
■ COLOR: predominantly black with varying amounts of white beneath, usually showing dorsally as a white patch at the front of the lower jaw. Patch often has several dark gray to black spots. There is often a light gray to white band around the tail stock, just in front of the flukes. The white on the tail expands with age, and large, old bowheads may have an almost completely white tail
■ BLOW: V-shaped blow

WHALE WATCHING
● WHEN TO GO: *June to September (Greenland); May to September (Baffin Island)*
● WHERE TO GO: *Greenland; Baffin Island, Nunavut, Canada*
● SURFACE BEHAVIOUR: *breaching, fluke slapping and often raising flukes when diving*

FAMILY BALAENOPTERIDAE

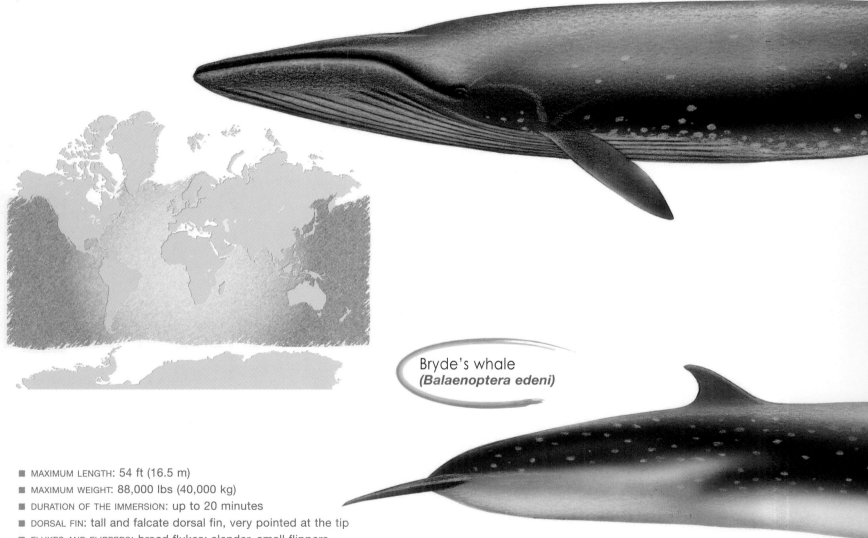

Minke whale
(*Balaenoptera acutorostrata*)

- MAXIMUM LENGTH: 32 ft (9.8 m)
- MAXIMUM WEIGHT: 20,000 lbs (9,200 kg)
- DURATION OF THE IMMERSION: up to 20 minutes
- DORSAL FIN: tall, curved dorsal fin
- FLUKES AND FLIPPERS: dark gray, narrow flippers with pointed tips; white band across the flippers
- HEAD: sharply pointed, V-shaped head
- COLOR: dark gray dorsally and white beneath, with streaks of intermediate shades on the sides
- BLOW: very fine and often not visible; disperses quickly

WHALE WATCHING

- WHEN TO GO: *April to October (Scotland); May to September (Iceland); March to July (Bay of Biscay); June to September (Greenland, Gulf of St. Lawrence, Glacier Bay)*
- WHERE TO GO: *found in all oceans. Sites include west coast of Scotland and Western Isles; Iceland; Bay of Biscay, Spain; Greenland; Gulf of St. Lawrence, Quebec, Canada; Glacier Bay, Alaska, USA*
- SURFACE BEHAVIOUR: *sometimes inquisitive and spyhops around smaller boats; breaching; does not raise flukes when diving*

Bryde's whale
(*Balaenoptera edeni*)

- MAXIMUM LENGTH: 54 ft (16.5 m)
- MAXIMUM WEIGHT: 88,000 lbs (40,000 kg)
- DURATION OF THE IMMERSION: up to 20 minutes
- DORSAL FIN: tall and falcate dorsal fin, very pointed at the tip
- FLUKES AND FLIPPERS: broad flukes; slender, small flippers
- HEAD: three parallel ridges on the rostrum; head shape is somewhat pointed; head makes up about 25 percent of body length
- COLOR: dark, smoky gray upperside and white underside
- BLOW: when visible, the blow can be either columnar or bushy, with variable height

WHALE WATCHING

- WHEN TO GO: *June to November (Hermanus); January-April (Baja California)*
- WHERE TO GO: *found in tropical to temperate waters worldwide. Sites include Australia; Sri Lanka; Hermanus, South Africa; Baja California, Mexico*
- SURFACE BEHAVIOUR: *frequently arches its back but does not raise flukes when diving; can be acrobatic and breaching several times in a row*

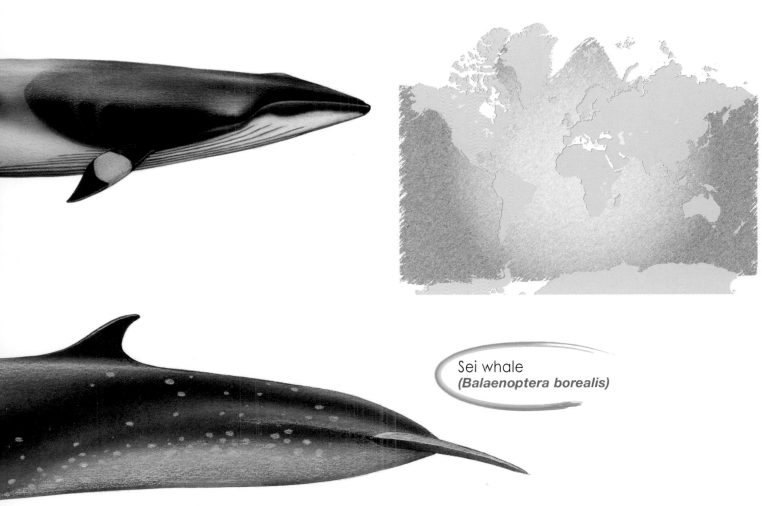

Sei whale
(Balaenoptera borealis)

- MAXIMUM LENGTH: 59 ft (18 m)
- MAXIMUM WEIGHT: 99,000 lbs (45,000 kg)
- DURATION OF THE IMMERSION: 5 to 20 minutes
- DORSAL FIN: large, prominent dorsal fin
- FLUKES AND FLIPPERS: short fins, pointed at the tips; relatively small flukes
- HEAD: pointed rostrum and a single longitudinal ridge on the rostrum; slightly arched head with a downturned tip
- COLOR: dark gray dorsally and often white or cream-colored on the underside. Oval scars often cover the body
- BLOW: tall, columnar blow

WHALE WATCHING

- *WHEN TO GO: late November to March (Antarctic Peninsula); June to November (Bay of Fundy)*
- *WHERE TO GO: distributed worldwide from subtropical or tropical waters to high latitudes. Seis are known worldwide for their unpredictable occurrences, with a sudden influx into an area followed by disappearance for years or even decades Sites include Antarctic Peninsula; Bay of Fundy, New Brunswick, Canada*
- *SURFACE BEHAVIOUR: elusive species; does not raise flukes when diving*

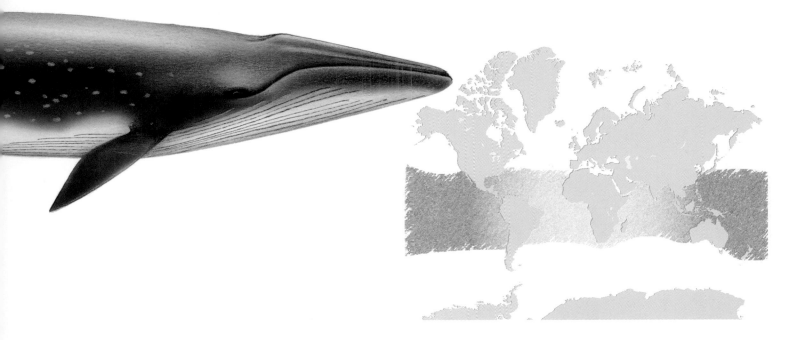

Fin whale
(*Balaenoptera physalus*)

- MAXIMUM LENGTH: 89 ft (27 m)
- MAXIMUM WEIGHT: 265,000 lbs (120,000 kg)
- DURATION OF THE IMMERSION: to 15 minutes, up to 30 minutes
- DEPTH OF THE IMMERSION: up to 750 ft (230 m)
- DORSAL FIN: small dorsal fin that is often pointed or falcate
- FLUKES AND FLIPPERS: long, tapered flippers; relatively small, triangular flukes
- HEAD: V-shaped and pointed head, with asymmetrical head pigmentation; the left lower jaw is mostly dark while the right jaw is largely white
- COLOR: dark above and white or cream-colored below
- BLOW: tall, narrow, vertical blow, up to 26 ft (8 m) high

WHALE WATCHING

- *WHEN TO GO: January to April (Baja California), December to March (Antarctica); March to July (Bay of Biscay); April to September (Ligurian Sea); June to September (Greenland); June to November (Gulf of St. Lawrence, Bay of Fundy); April to October (New England)*
- *WHERE TO GO: Cosmopolitan species that occurs in all major oceans usually in temperate to polar latitudes and less commonly in the tropics. Sites include Baja California, Mexico; Antarctic Peninsula; Bay of Biscay, Spain; Ligurian Sea, France/Italy; Greenland; Gulf of St. Lawrence, Quebec, Canada; Bay of Fundy, New Brunswick, Canada; Maine, New Hampshire, and Massachusetts, New England, USA*
- *SURFACE BEHAVIOUR: rarely raises flukes when diving*

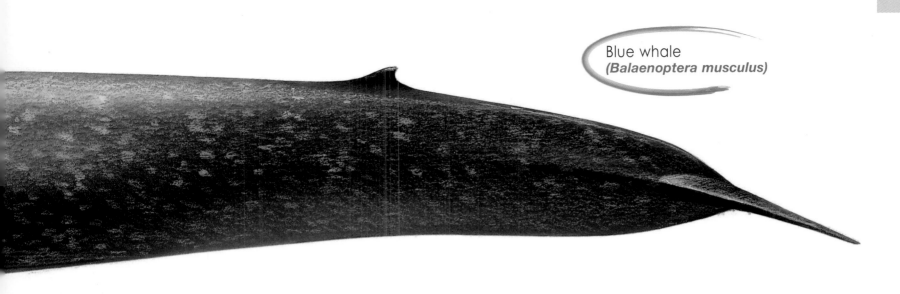

- ■ MAXIMUM LENGTH: 108 ft (33 m)
- ■ MAXIMUM WEIGHT: 400,000 (180,000 kg)
- ■ DURATION OF THE IMMERSION: up to 30 minutes
- ■ DEPTH OF THE IMMERSION: up to 656 ft (200 m)
- ■ DORSAL FIN: small dorsal fin set well back on body
- ■ FLUKES AND FLIPPERS: long and pointed flippers; broad, triangular flukes
- ■ HEAD: large, U-shaped head, up to one-fourth of total body length
- ■ COLOR: bluish-gray dorsally and lighter underneath; the head is uniformly blue, but the back and sides are mottled blue and light gray. Light to extensive mottling on the sides, back, and belly. The patterns of mottling are used to identify individuals
- ■ BLOW: tall and columnar, reaching up to 40 ft (12 m), the highest of any whale

WHALE WATCHING

- ● *WHEN TO GO: June to November (Gulf of St. Lawrence); August to October (Monterey Bay); January to April (Baja California)*
- ● *WHERE TO GO: Gulf of St. Lawrence, Quebec, Canada; Monterey Bay, California, USA; Baja California, Mexico*
- ● *SURFACE BEHAVIOUR: often raises flukes when diving; on sunny days body below surface appears as turquoise silhouette*

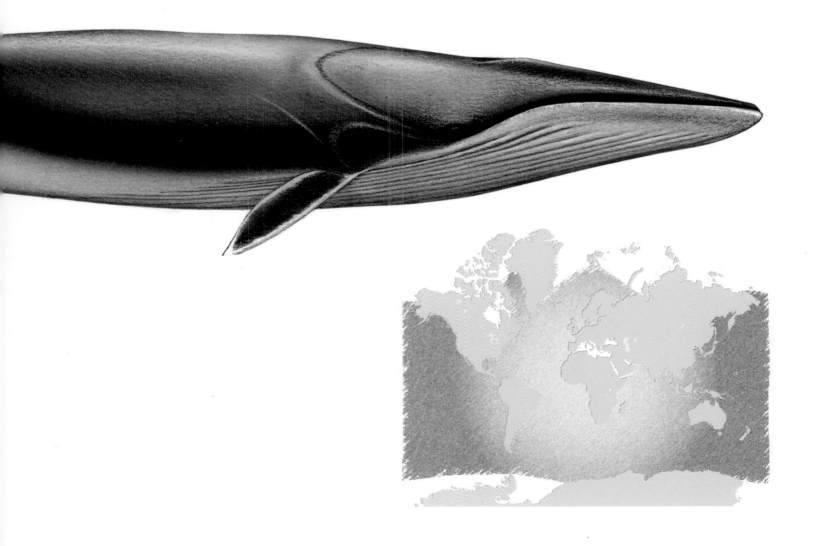

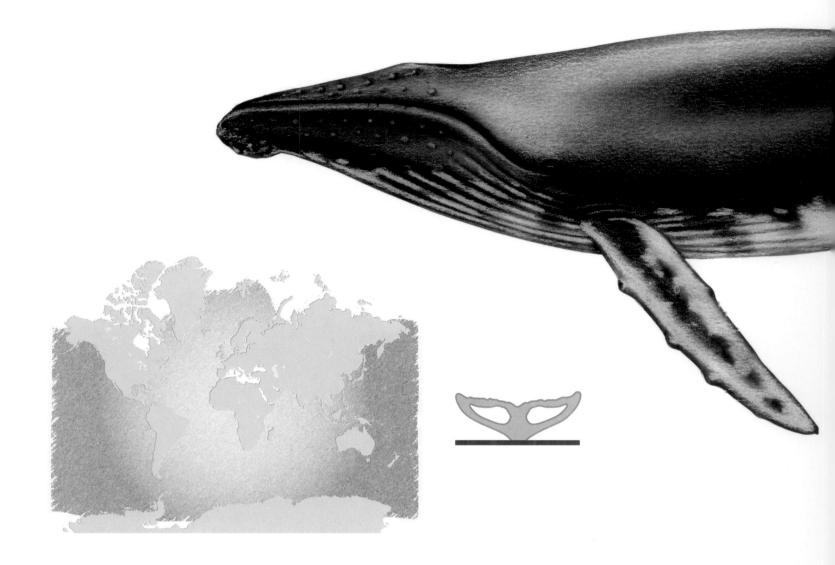

FAMILY ESCHRICHTIIDAE

Gray whale
(Eschrichtius robustus)

- ■ MAXIMUM LENGTH: 50 ft (15 m)
- ■ MAXIMUM WEIGHT: 99,000 lbs (45,000 kg)
- ■ DURATION OF THE IMMERSION: up to 25 minutes
- ■ DEPTH OF THE IMMERSION: 560 ft (170 m)
- ■ DORSAL FIN: no dorsal fin, but a dorsal hump followed by 6 to 12 bumps or "knuckles" on the dorsal ridge of the tail stock
- ■ FLUKES AND FLIPPERS: broad and paddle-shaped flippers, with pointed tips; wide flukes that are over 3 m across in adults
- ■ HEAD: triangular-shaped head; slightly arched mouth line
- ■ COLOR: grey body, marbled and scarred with numerous barnacles and encrusted small parasitic crustaceans
- ■ BLOW: low heart- or V-shaped blow, up to 13 ft (4 m) high

WHALE WATCHING

- ● *WHEN TO GO: January to April (Baja California); March to April (Vancouver Island); December to May (Monterey Bay)*
- ● *WHERE TO GO: lagoons of Baja California, Mexico; Vancouver Island, British Columbia; Monterey Bay, California, USA*
- ● *SURFACE BEHAVIOUR: can be demonstrative, inquisitive and friendly; may approach boats; breaching, lobtailing, spyhopping and raising flukes high when diving*

248

Humpback whale
(*Megaptera novaeangliae*)

- ■ MAXIMUM LENGTH: 56 ft (17 m)
- ■ MAXIMUM WEIGHT: 88,000 lbs (40,000 kg)
- ■ DURATION OF THE IMMERSION: 3 to 15 minutes; up to 40 minutes
- ■ DEPTH OF THE IMMERSION: up to 490 ft (150 m)
- ■ DORSAL FIN: varies in size and shape, from small triangular knob to larger sickle: situated nearly two-thirds back along the body on small hump
- ■ FLUKES AND FLIPPERS: extremely long arm-like flippers that are one-third the body length; white below and white or black above; flukes have a serrated trailing edge and a black and white color pattern
- ■ HEAD: slender and flat head covered with a variable number of rounded protuberances, called tubercles
- ■ COLOR: black upperside; white, black or mottled underside
- ■ BLOW: low and broad but highly visible reaching up to 10 ft (3 m)

WHALE WATCHING

- ● *WHEN TO GO: December to March (Hawaii); April to October (British Columbia); January to April (Baja California; Silver Bank); December to March (Antarctic peninsula); June to November (Gulf of St. Lawrence, Bay of Fundy); April to October (New England); June to September (Glacier Bay); July to November (Hervey Bay)*
- ● *WHERE TO GO: found in all major oceans. Sites include: Monterey Bay, California, USA; Baja California, Mexico; Hawaii; British Columbia coast, Canada; Antarctic Peninsula; Hervey Bay, Queensland, Australia; Silver Bank, Dominican Republic; Gulf of St. Lawrence, Quebec, Canada; Bay of Fundy, New Brunswick, Canada; New England, USA; Glacier Bay, Alaska*
- ● *SURFACE BEHAVIOUR: known for energetic and acrobatic behaviors including breaching, spyhopping, lobtailing and tail- and flipper-slapping. Flukes often lifted very high prior to diving*

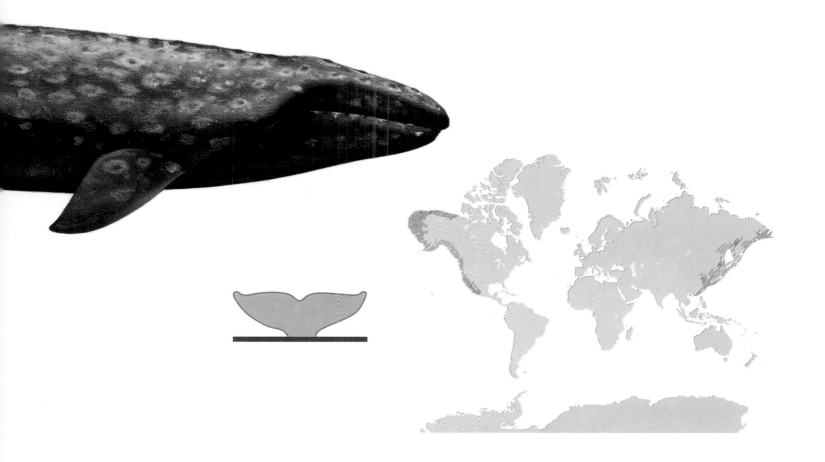

Odontoceti
FAMILY DELPHINIDAE

Commerson's dolphin
(Cephalorhynchus commersonii)

- MAXIMUM LENGTH: 6 ft (1.8 m)
- MAXIMUM WEIGHT: 190 lbs (86 kg)
- DURATION OF THE IMMERSION: 15 to 20 seconds
- DORSAL FIN: small, rounded dorsal fin, rising at a shallow angle from the back, and leaning slightly towards the tail
- FLUKES AND FLIPPERS: flippers and flukes have rounded tips
- HEAD: conical blunt head with gently sloping forehead and little or no beak
- COLOR: largely white, except black face, flippers, dorsal fin, and flukes

WHALE WATCHING
- *WHEN TO GO:* ***December to March***
- *WHERE TO GO:* ***common off Patagonia, Tierra del Fuego, Argentina, and the Falkland Islands***
- *SURFACE BEHAVIOUR:* ***fast, active swimmer; frequently bow-rides, swimming upside-down or spinning underwater; breaches and leaps***

Heaviside's dolphin
(Cephalorhynchus heavisidii)

- MAXIMUM LENGTH: 5.5 ft (1.7 m)
- MAXIMUM WEIGHT: 246 lbs (75 kg)
- DORSAL FIN: triangular and pointed
- FLUKES AND FLIPPERS: flukes distinctly notched with pointed tips; small flippers with blunt tips
- HEAD: cone-shaped head with indistinct beak; dark oval area around eye
- COLOR: largely grey, with blackish-blue cape which starts at the blowhole; light gray thoracic region; white ventral patch

WHALE WATCHING
- *WHEN TO GO:* ***year-round***
- *WHERE TO GO:* ***Namibia; west coast of South Africa in Cape Town region***
- *SURFACE BEHAVIOUR:* ***seen in small groups of 10 or fewer animals; quick and agile; bowriding; leaping out of the water***

Hector's dolphin
(Cephalorhynchus hectori)

- MAXIMUM LENGTH: 5 ft (1.5 m)
- MAXIMUM WEIGHT: 125 lbs (57 kg)
- DORSAL FIN: low, broad, rounded dorsal fin
- FLUKES AND FLIPPERS: rounded and paddle-shaped flippers, with blunt tips
- HEAD: blunt head with black, non-protruding beak
- COLOR: predominantly light gray; dorsal fin, flukes, flippers, area around the blowhole, and much of the face are dark gray to black

WHALE WATCHING

- *WHEN TO GO:* **October to May**
- *WHERE TO GO:* **Banks Peninsula, South Island, New Zealand; boat trips leave from Akaroa Harbour**
- *SURFACE BEHAVIOUR:* **active, acrobatic; leaping out of water; bowriding**

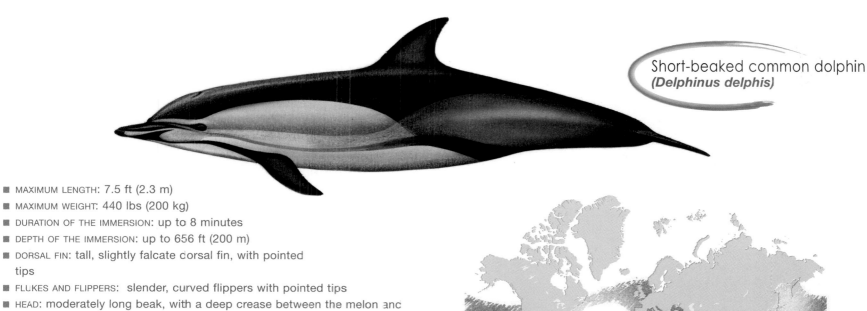

Short-beaked common dolphin
(Delphinus delphis)

- MAXIMUM LENGTH: 7.5 ft (2.3 m)
- MAXIMUM WEIGHT: 440 lbs (200 kg)
- DURATION OF THE IMMERSION: up to 8 minutes
- DEPTH OF THE IMMERSION: up to 656 ft (200 m)
- DORSAL FIN: tall, slightly falcate dorsal fin, with pointed tips
- FLUKES AND FLIPPERS: slender, curved flippers with pointed tips
- HEAD: moderately long beak, with a deep crease between the melon and beak; rounded, bulging melon
- COLOR: dark brownish-gray back; white belly; tan to ochre thoracic patch; the thoracic patch is light, contrasting strongly with the dark cape.

WHALE WATCHING

- *WHEN TO GO:* **March to September**
- *WHERE TO GO:* **Baja California, Mexico**
- *SURFACE BEHAVIOUR:* **active and energetic bowrider; rides the "bow waves" of large whales; often performing various breaches and leaps; highly vocal; squeals can be heard above the surface while bowriding**

Short-finned pilot whale
(Globicephala macrorhynchus)

- MAXIMUM LENGTH: 24 ft (7.5 m)
- MAXIMUM WEIGHT: 7,900 lbs (3,600 kg)
- DURATION OF THE IMMERSION: up to 27 minutes
- DEPTH OF THE IMMERSION: up to 3,000 ft (900 m)
- DORSAL FIN: low, falcate dorsal fin
- FLUKES AND FLIPPERS: long and sickle-shaped flippers
- HEAD: bulbous head, very short or non-existent beak
- COLOR: black to dark brownish-gray body, with a light gray patch on the chest and a gray saddle patch behind the fin
- BLOW: strong blow up to 4 ft (1.2 m) high

WHALE WATCHING

- WHEN TO GO: *March to November*
- WHERE TO GO: *La Gomera, Canary Islands*
- SURFACE BEHAVIOUR: *pods of up to several hundreds of short-finned pilot whales are seen; members of this highly social species are almost never seen alone; individuals sometimes spyhop*

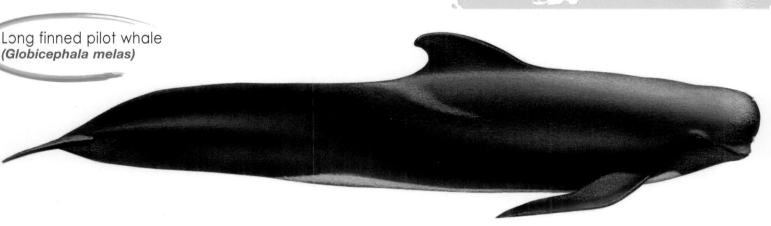

Long finned pilot whale
(Globicephala melas)

- MAXIMUM LENGTH: 22 ft (6.7 m)
- MAXIMUM WEIGHT: 5,100 lbs (2,300 kg)
- DURATION OF THE IMMERSION: 10 to 16 minutes
- DEPTH OF THE IMMERSION: 100 to 200 ft (30 to 60 m), up to 2,000 ft (600 m)
- DORSAL FIN: low, falcate dorsal fin located about a third of the way back from the snout tip
- FLUKES AND FLIPPERS: extremely long and slender flippers with pointed tips; flukes have concave trailing edges and a distinct notch
- HEAD: males have larger, more bulbous heads than females; short beak
- COLOR: predominantly dark gray, brown, or black body, with a white to light gray patch on the chest and a light gray saddle patch behind the dorsal fin
- BLOW: strong blow up to 4 ft (1.2 m) high

WHALE WATCHING

- WHEN TO GO: *May to September*
- WHERE TO GO: *Ligurian Sea, between France and Italy*
- SURFACE BEHAVIOUR: *often seen rafting in groups at the surface, apparently resting; commonly spyhops and lobtails*

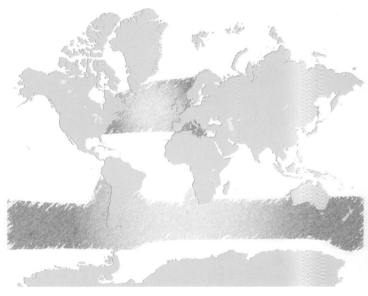

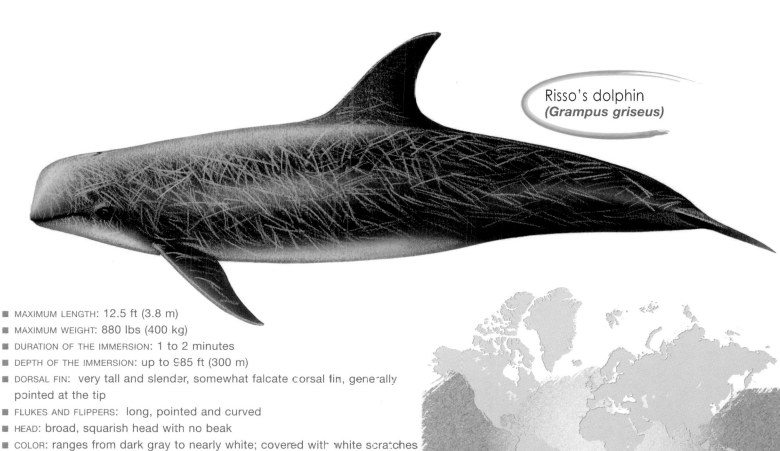

Risso's dolphin
(Grampus griseus)

- MAXIMUM LENGTH: 12.5 ft (3.8 m)
- MAXIMUM WEIGHT: 880 lbs (400 kg)
- DURATION OF THE IMMERSION: 1 to 2 minutes
- DEPTH OF THE IMMERSION: up to 985 ft (300 m)
- DORSAL FIN: very tall and slender, somewhat falcate dorsal fin, generally pointed at the tip
- FLUKES AND FLIPPERS: long, pointed and curved
- HEAD: broad, squarish head with no beak
- COLOR: ranges from dark gray to nearly white; covered with white scratches and spots, thought to result from squid, their major prey, and other Risso's dolphins; this species is the most heavily-scarred of all dolphins

WHALE WATCHING

- *WHEN TO GO: year-round*
- *WHERE TO GO: Maldives; Sri Lanka; Azores*
- *SURFACE BEHAVIOUR: sometimes breaching, spyhopping, porpoising, and occasionally bowriding*

Atlantic white-sided dolphin
(Lagenorhynchus acutus)

- MAXIMUM LENGTH: 9 ft (2.8 m)
- MAXIMUM WEIGHT: 520 lbs (236 kg)
- DORSAL FIN: black, tall, strongly sickle-shaped dorsal fin
- FLUKES AND FLIPPERS: black flippers with pointed tips; flukes have concave trailing edges and a notch in the middle
- HEAD: very short stubby beak with black upper jaw
- COLOR: complex and striking color pattern; upper back is black or dark gray with a white patch and a yellow or tan patch just below the middle of each flank is gray and the lower part and underside are predominantly white

WHALE WATCHING

- *WHEN TO GO: April to October*
- *WHERE TO GO: Massachusetts, USA; boat trips live from various towns including Gloucester, Provincetown, Plymouth, and Nantucket*
- *SURFACE BEHAVIOUR: live and acrobatic, often breaching and tail-slapping*

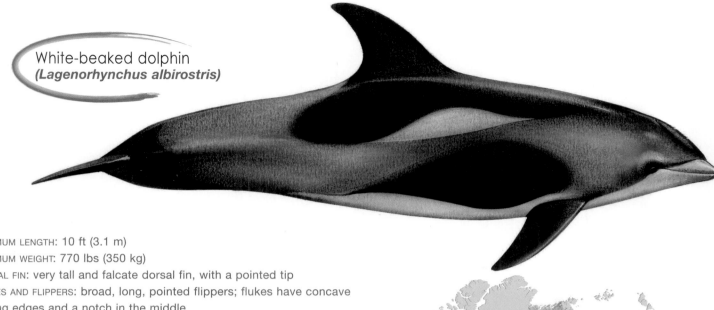

White-beaked dolphin
(Lagenorhynchus albirostris)

- MAXIMUM LENGTH: 10 ft (3.1 m)
- MAXIMUM WEIGHT: 770 lbs (350 kg)
- DORSAL FIN: very tall and falcate dorsal fin, with a pointed tip
- FLUKES AND FLIPPERS: broad, long, pointed flippers; flukes have concave trailing edges and a notch in the middle
- HEAD: short and thick beak that is usually white, set-off from the melon by a shallow crease
- COLOR: mostly black to dark gray on the upper sides and back; beak and most of the belly are white to light gray, and often mottled; light streaks may surround the eye; dorsal fin, flippers, and flukes are mostly dark

WHALE WATCHING

- *WHEN TO GO: **May to September***
- *WHERE TO GO: **Húsavík, Keflavik, Olafsvik, Reykjavik, Iceland; Western Isles, Scotland***
- *SURFACE BEHAVIOUR: **active, often leaping and breaching; approaches vessels to ride bow or stern waves***

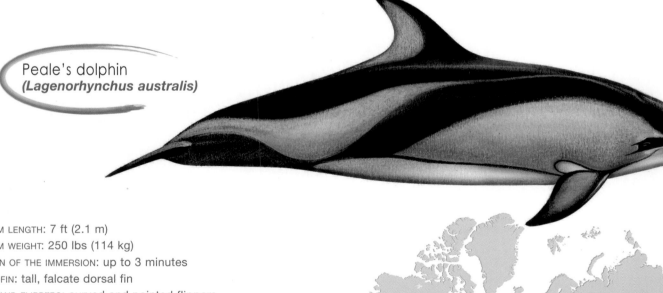

Peale's dolphin
(Lagenorhynchus australis)

- MAXIMUM LENGTH: 7 ft (2.1 m)
- MAXIMUM WEIGHT: 250 lbs (114 kg)
- DURATION OF THE IMMERSION: up to 3 minutes
- DORSAL FIN: tall, falcate dorsal fin
- FLUKES AND FLIPPERS: curved and pointed flippers
- HEAD: short, stubby beak
- COLOR: grayish-black above and white below; flippers are gray-black, and the dorsal fin is dark gray-black, with a thin crescent of light gray on the trailing margin; the beak tip, lips, and entire lower jaw are dark gray to black

WHALE WATCHING

- *WHEN TO GO: **year-round***
- *WHERE TO GO: **Patagonia; Falkland Islands***
- *SURFACE BEHAVIOUR: **commonly breaches, spyhops, and slaps head, flukes and flippers on the surface; frequently bowrides; at the bow, often speeds ahead, leaps high into the air and falls back into the water on its sides***

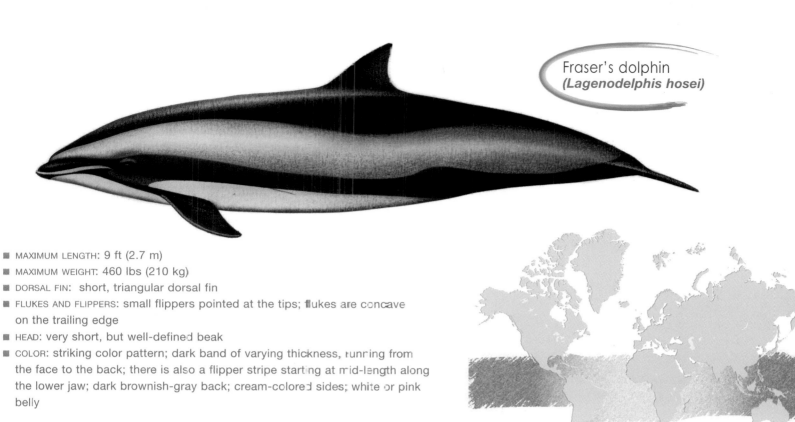

Fraser's dolphin
(*Lagenodelphis hosei*)

- MAXIMUM LENGTH: 9 ft (2.7 m)
- MAXIMUM WEIGHT: 460 lbs (210 kg)
- DORSAL FIN: short, triangular dorsal fin
- FLUKES AND FLIPPERS: small flippers pointed at the tips; flukes are concave on the trailing edge
- HEAD: very short, but well-defined beak
- COLOR: striking color pattern; dark band of varying thickness, running from the face to the back; there is also a flipper stripe starting at mid-length along the lower jaw; dark brownish-gray back; cream-colored sides; white or pink belly

WHALE WATCHING

- *WHEN TO GO: year-round*
- *WHERE TO GO: Maldives*
- *SURFACE BEHAVIOUR: active and often seen in dense schools of hundreds or even thousands of dolphins; shy and difficult to approach*

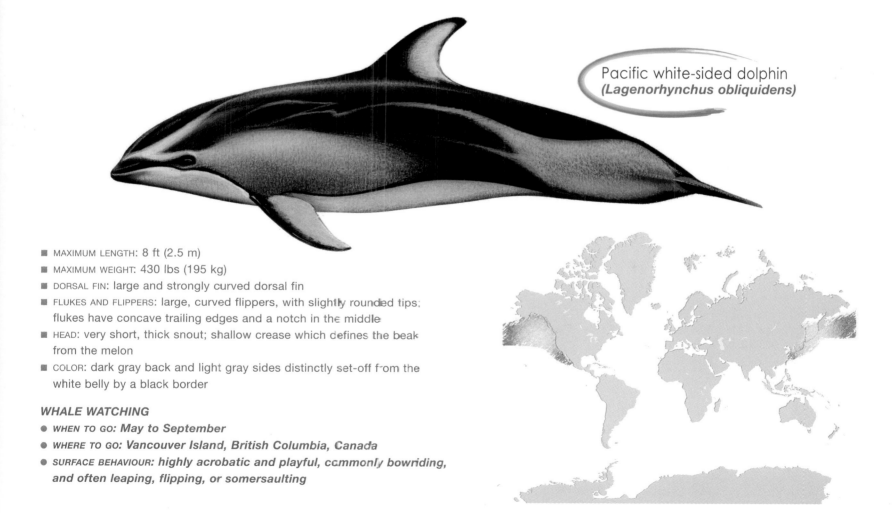

Pacific white-sided dolphin
(*Lagenorhynchus obliquidens*)

- MAXIMUM LENGTH: 8 ft (2.5 m)
- MAXIMUM WEIGHT: 430 lbs (195 kg)
- DORSAL FIN: large and strongly curved dorsal fin
- FLUKES AND FLIPPERS: large, curved flippers, with slightly rounded tips; flukes have concave trailing edges and a notch in the middle
- HEAD: very short, thick snout; shallow crease which defines the beak from the melon
- COLOR: dark gray back and light gray sides distinctly set-off from the white belly by a black border

WHALE WATCHING

- *WHEN TO GO: May to September*
- *WHERE TO GO: Vancouver Island, British Columbia, Canada*
- *SURFACE BEHAVIOUR: highly acrobatic and playful, commonly bowriding, and often leaping, flipping, or somersaulting*

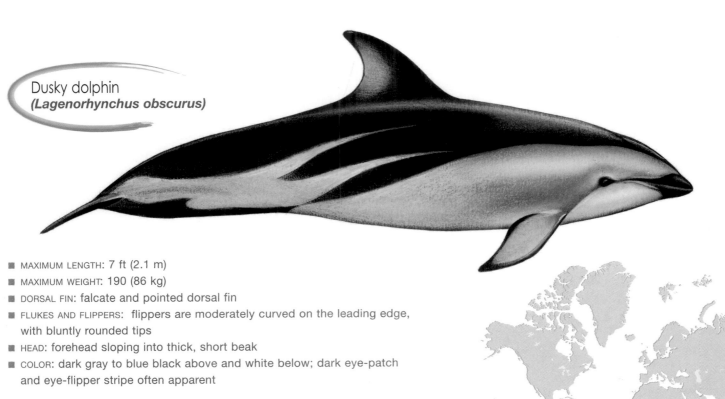

Dusky dolphin
(*Lagenorhynchus obscurus*)

- ■ MAXIMUM LENGTH: 7 ft (2.1 m)
- ■ MAXIMUM WEIGHT: 190 (86 kg)
- ■ DORSAL FIN: falcate and pointed dorsal fin
- ■ FLUKES AND FLIPPERS: flippers are moderately curved on the leading edge, with bluntly rounded tips
- ■ HEAD: forehead sloping into thick, short beak
- ■ COLOR: dark gray to blue black above and white below; dark eye-patch and eye-flipper stripe often apparent

WHALE WATCHING

- ● *WHEN TO GO:* **year-round**
- ● *WHERE TO GO:* **Kaikoura, New Zealand**
- ● *SURFACE BEHAVIOUR:* **one of the most acrobatic of all dolphins, frequently leaping out of the water with high jumps and twists; may leap several dozen times, with entire group following the first to breach; readily approaches vessels to engage in bowriding; highly gregarious**

Northern right whale dolphin
(*Lissodelphis borealis*)

- ■ MAXIMUM LENGTH: 10 ft (3.1 m)
- ■ MAXIMUM WEIGHT: 253 lbs (115 kg)
- ■ DURATION OF THE IMMERSION: 253 lbs (115 kg)
- ■ DORSAL FIN: no dorsal fin
- ■ FLUKES AND FLIPPERS: flukes and flippers are small and narrow
- ■ HEAD: short, but well-defined beak
- ■ COLOR: black, with a distinctly-bordered white band from the throat to the fluke notch that widens to cover the entire area between the flippers, and a white patch just behind the tip of the lower jaw; the trailing edges of the flukes have a crescent-shaped patch of light gray edging above and white below

WHALE WATCHING

- ● *WHEN TO GO:* **April to October**
- ● *WHERE TO GO:* **Monterey Bay, California, USA**
- ● *SURFACE BEHAVIOUR:* **travels in groups; bowrides especially when accompanied by other species of dolphins; may perform breaches and side-slaps**

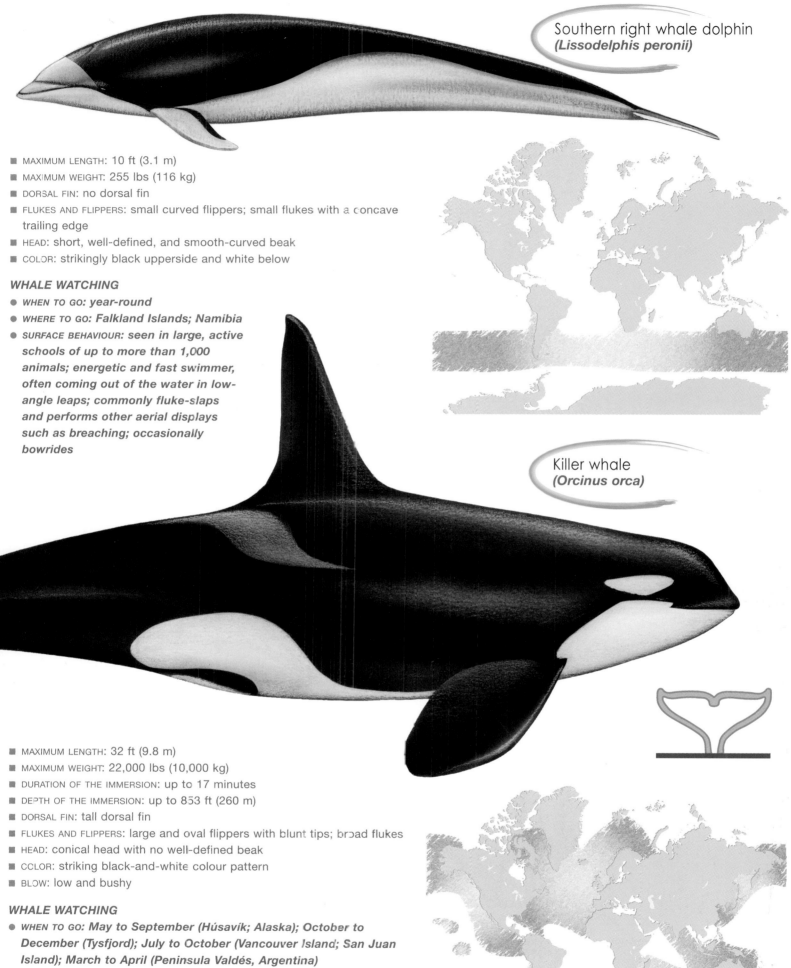

Southern right whale dolphin
(Lissodelphis peronii)

- MAXIMUM LENGTH: 10 ft (3.1 m)
- MAXIMUM WEIGHT: 255 lbs (116 kg)
- DORSAL FIN: no dorsal fin
- FLUKES AND FLIPPERS: small curved flippers; small flukes with a concave trailing edge
- HEAD: short, well-defined, and smooth-curved beak
- COLOR: strikingly black upperside and white below

WHALE WATCHING

- *WHEN TO GO: year-round*
- *WHERE TO GO: Falkland Islands; Namibia*
- *SURFACE BEHAVIOUR: seen in large, active schools of up to more than 1,000 animals; energetic and fast swimmer, often coming out of the water in low-angle leaps; commonly fluke-slaps and performs other aerial displays such as breaching; occasionally bowrides*

Killer whale
(Orcinus orca)

- MAXIMUM LENGTH: 32 ft (9.8 m)
- MAXIMUM WEIGHT: 22,000 lbs (10,000 kg)
- DURATION OF THE IMMERSION: up to 17 minutes
- DEPTH OF THE IMMERSION: up to 853 ft (260 m)
- DORSAL FIN: tall dorsal fin
- FLUKES AND FLIPPERS: large and oval flippers with blunt tips; broad flukes
- HEAD: conical head with no well-defined beak
- COLOR: striking black-and-white colour pattern
- BLOW: low and bushy

WHALE WATCHING

- *WHEN TO GO: May to September (Húsavík; Alaska); October to December (Tysfjord); July to October (Vancouver Island; San Juan Island); March to April (Peninsula Valdés, Argentina)*
- *WHERE TO GO: the most cosmopolitan of all cetaceans. Sites include: Húsavík, Iceland; Tysfjord, Norway; Vancouver Island, British Columbia, Canada; San Juan Island, Washington, USA; Peninsula Valdés, Patagonia, Argentina; Glacier Bay, Alaska*
- *SURFACE BEHAVIOUR: may breach, spyhop, flipper-slap and fluke-slap*

WHERE AND WHAT TO WATCH

257

Irrawaddy dolphin
(*Orcaella brevirostris*)

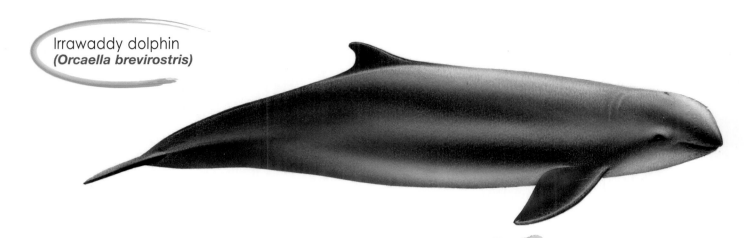

- MAXIMUM LENGTH: 9 ft (2.75 m)
- MAXIMUM WEIGHT: 286 (130 kg)
- DURATION OF THE IMMERSION: most dives are fewer than 3 minutes long; up to 12 minutes)
- DORSAL FIN: small, rounded dorsal fin, set just behind mid-back
- FLUKES AND FLIPPERS: large paddle-shaped flippers with curved leading edges and rounded tips; small, notched flukes
- HEAD: blunt and bulbous head with no beak; straight mouth line angled upward, with "smiling" appearance
- COLOR: back and sides of the body are gray to bluish-gray; the belly is lighter

WHALE WATCHING

- *WHERE TO GO: inhabits coastal and shallow waters, including lagoons, river mouths and freshwater rivers. Sites include Sarawak, Malaysia; Mekong River, Cambodia*
- *SURFACE BEHAVIOUR: shy and not particularly active; does not bowride, but occasionally makes low leaps, breaches, and spyhops*

Melon-headed whale
(*Peponocephala electra*)

- MAXIMUM LENGTH: 9 ft (2.7 m)
- MAXIMUM WEIGHT: 460 lbs (210 kg)
- DORSAL FIN: tall and slightly falcate, located near the middle of the back
- FLUKES AND FLIPPERS: sickle-shaped flippers with pointed tips
- HEAD: small head, with little or no beak and a rounded melon
- COLOR: charcoal gray to nearly black body, with variable light gray or white ventral markings and often light gray, pink or white lips

WHALE WATCHING

- *WHEN TO GO: year-round*
- *WHERE TO GO: Tanon Strait, Philippines; Hawaii*
- *SURFACE BEHAVIOUR: highly gregarious species, commonly seen in large schools of rafting individuals in resting formation; often moves at high speed porpoising out of the water; eager bowrider, often displacing other species from the bow wave*

False killer whale
(Pseudorca crassidens)

- MAXIMUM LENGTH: 20 ft (6 m)
- MAXIMUM WEIGHT: 4,400 lbs (2,000 kg)
- DEPTH OF THE IMMERSION: up to 1,600 ft (500 m)
- DORSAL FIN: falcate and slender dorsal fin, generally rounded at the tip
- FLUKES AND FLIPPERS: flippers with rounded tips and a characteristic hump on the leading edge, which gives the flippers the appearance of an S-shape
- HEAD: rounded overhanging melon and no discernable beak
- COLOR: dark gray to black body, with a light gray patch on the chest, and sometimes light gray areas on the head
- BLOW: indistinct

WHALE WATCHING

- *WHEN TO GO: **year-round***
- *WHERE TO GO: **Hawaii***
- *SURFACE BEHAVIOUR: **rides bow waves of vessels; commonly breaches***

Tucuxi
(Sotalia fluviatilis)

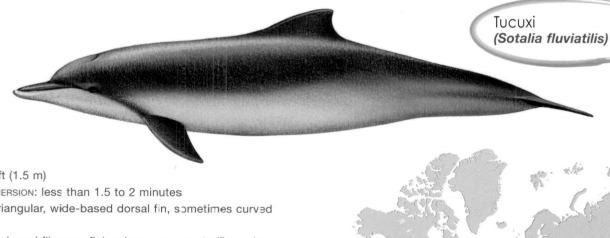

- MAXIMUM LENGTH: 5 ft (1.5 m)
- DURATION OF THE IMMERSION: less than 1.5 to 2 minutes
- DORSAL FIN: short, triangular, wide-based dorsal fin, sometimes curved at the tip
- FLUKES AND FLIPPERS: broad flippers; flukes have concave trailing edges and a notch in the middle
- HEAD: rounded melon; long and narrow beak
- COLOR: dark-bluish or brownish gray on the upperside; light gray or white with a pinkish tinge on the belly; broad, poorly-defined stripe from the eye to the flipper; flippers and flukes are dark gray on the underside

WHALE WATCHING

- *WHEN TO GO: **June to October***
- *WHERE TO GO: **almost exclusively freshwater species; found in the Amazon River; boat trips depart from ports on Santa Catarina Island, Brazil***
- *SURFACE BEHAVIOUR: **shy and difficult to approach; can be acrobatic; frequently spyhops, lobtails, flipper-slaps, leaps, and breaches***

Indo-Pacific humpback dolphin and Atlantic humpback dolphin
(Sousa chinensis/Sousa teuszii)

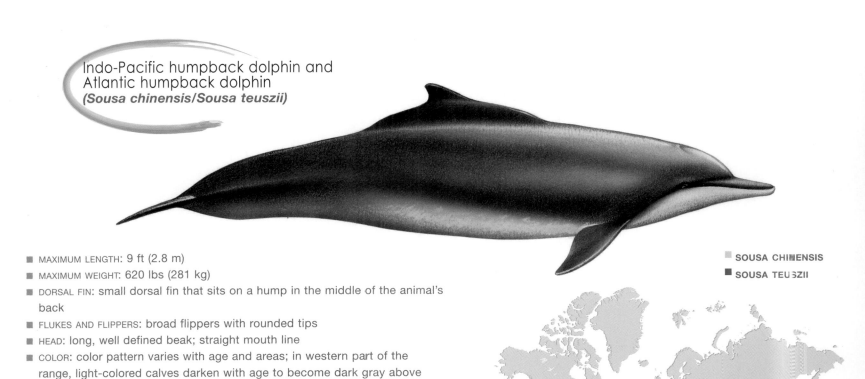

- MAXIMUM LENGTH: 9 ft (2.8 m)
- MAXIMUM WEIGHT: 620 lbs (281 kg)
- DORSAL FIN: small dorsal fin that sits on a hump in the middle of the animal's back
- FLUKES AND FLIPPERS: broad flippers with rounded tips
- HEAD: long, well defined beak; straight mouth line
- COLOR: color pattern varies with age and areas; in western part of the range, light-colored calves darken with age to become dark gray above and light gray below; in the eastern Indian and Pacific oceans, dark gray calves lighten with age, and become pinkish-white, often with spots (Indo-Pacific); typically gray on the sides and back, and light gray to whitish below (Atlantic)

WHALE WATCHING
- WHEN TO GO: *year-round*
- WHERE TO GO: *Western Cape, South Africa; Queensland, Australia; Hong Kong (Indo-Pacific)*
- SURFACE BEHAVIOUR: *bowriding is rare; shy of boats; moderately acrobatic*

□ SOUSA CHINENSIS
■ SOUSA TEUSZII

Pantropical spotted dolphin
(Stenella attenuata)

- MAXIMUM LENGTH: 8.5 ft (2.6 m)
- MAXIMUM WEIGHT: 260 lbs (118 kg)
- DORSAL FIN: narrow, falcate dorsal fin, pointed at the tip
- FLUKES AND FLIPPERS: slender and strongly curved flippers; flukes have swept-back leading edges and fairly straight trailing edges curved at the ends; there is a notch in the middle
- HEAD: long, slender beak separated from the melon by a distinct crease
- COLOR: dark dorsal cape; although unspotted at birth, by adulthood dolphins have varying degrees of white mottling on the dark cape

WHALE WATCHING
- WHEN TO GO: *year-round*
- WHERE TO GO: *Hawaii, USA*
- SURFACE BEHAVIOUR: *highly gregarious; fast swimmer; often engaging in acrobatics such as breaching and side slapping; frequently bowrides*

Striped dolphin
(Stenella coeruleoalba)

- ■ MAXIMUM LENGTH: 8 ft (2.5 m)
- ■ MAXIMUM WEIGHT: 345 lbs (157 kg)
- ■ DEPTH OF THE IMMERSION: up to 2,300 ft (700 m)
- ■ DORSAL FIN: tall and falcate
- ■ FLUKES AND FLIPPERS: curved and pointed flippers; flukes have slender blades and acutely rounded tips
- ■ HEAD: moderately long beak, with a distinct crease between the melon and beak
- ■ COLOR: upper body is gray or grown, with pale gray extending up from the middle flank toward the dorsal fin and across the rear body; a thin, dark stripe extends from the beak, around the eye, and along the lower flank, where it widens; a shorter stripe extends from the eye to the flipper; bely is white or pink

WHALE WATCHING
- ● WHEN TO GO: *April to September*
- ● WHERE TO GO: *Ligurian Sea, between France and Italy*
- ● SURFACE BEHAVIOUR: *fast swimmer; very acrobatic, performing frequent breaches and other aerial behaviors; often ride bow waves*

Atlantic spotted dolhpin
(Stenella frontalis)

- ■ MAXIMUM LENGTH: 7.5 ft (2.3 m)
- ■ MAXIMUM WEIGHT: 315 lbs (143 kg)
- ■ DORSAL FIN: tall and falcate dorsal fin
- ■ FLUKES AND FLIPPERS: curved flippers; flukes have swept-back leading edges and fairly straight trailing edges curved at the ends; there is a notch in the middle
- ■ HEAD: moderately long, stocky beak with a distinct crease between the melon and beak
- ■ COLOR: unspotted at birth; young animals look like bottlenose dolphins, with a dark cape, light gray sides, and white belly; spots develop on both dorsal and ventral surfaces as animals age

WHALE WATCHING
- ● WHEN TO GO: *May to September*
- ● WHERE TO GO: *Grand Bahama Island, Bahamas*
- ● SURFACE BEHAVIOUR: *highly gregarious; acrobatic; avid bowrider; typically leaping out of water and falling back with large splash*

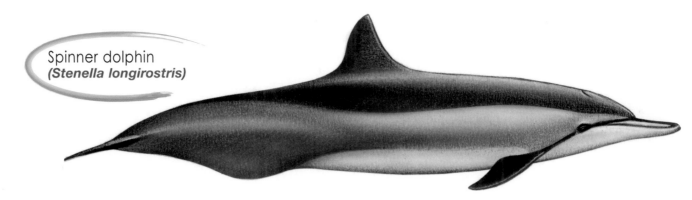

Spinner dolphin
(Stenella longirostris)

- MAXIMUM LENGTH: 8 ft (2.5 m)
- MAXIMUM WEIGHT: 180 lbs (82 kg)
- DEPTH OF THE IMMERSION: up to 1,970 ft (600 m)
- DORSAL FIN: ranges from slightly falcate to erect and triangular
- FLUKES AND FLIPPERS: slender and curved flippers; flukes have swept-back leading edges and straight trailing edges curved at the ends, with a notch in the middle
- HEAD: extremely long, thin beak; slender head
- COLOR: dark eye-to-flipper stripes and dark lips and beak tips; three-part color pattern, with dark gray cape, light gray sides, and white belly

WHALE WATCHING

- WHEN TO GO: *year-round*
- WHERE TO GO: *Hawaii, USA; Tanon Strait, Philippines; Caribbean*
- SURFACE BEHAVIOUR: *one of the most aerial of all dolphins; often performs breaches, side-slaps, fluke-slaps, and spins; active bowriders*

Common bottlenose dolphin
(Tursiops truncatus)

- MAXIMUM LENGTH: 12.5 ft (3.8 m)
- MAXIMUM WEIGHT: 1,430 lbs (649 kg)
- DURATION OF THE IMMERSION: 3 to 4 minutes
- DORSAL FIN: tall and falcate dorsal fin, set near the middle of the back
- FLUKES AND FLIPPERS: curved and pointed at the tips; flukes have a notch in the middle, swept-back leading edges, and straight trailing edges that are curved at the ends
- HEAD: short beak that is distinctly set off from the melon by a crease; gently-curved mouth line that dips down from the tip of the beak, then back up, and finally down again at the gape, giving the dolphin a "smiling" appearance
- COLOR: varies from light gray to nearly black on the back and sides, fading to white on the belly

WHALE WATCHING

- WHEN TO GO: *year-round for most locations*
- WHERE TO GO: *very widely distributed. Sites include: Monkey Mia, Shark Bay, Australia; Western Isles, Scotland; Azores; Hawaii, USA; Caribbean*
- SURFACE BEHAVIOUR: *avid bowrider; may perform acrobatic leaps while bowriding; active when feeding or socializing, often slapping the water with flukes, leaping, and performing other aerial behaviors*

FAMILY INIIDAE

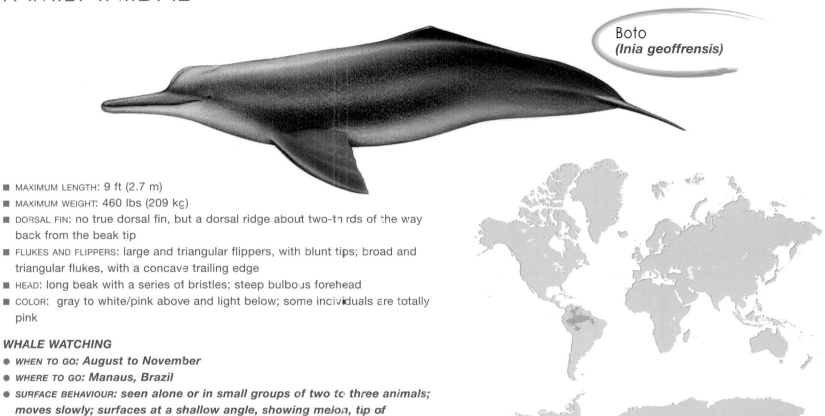

Boto
(Inia geoffrensis)

- MAXIMUM LENGTH: 9 ft (2.7 m)
- MAXIMUM WEIGHT: 460 lbs (209 kg)
- DORSAL FIN: no true dorsal fin, but a dorsal ridge about two-thirds of the way back from the beak tip
- FLUKES AND FLIPPERS: large and triangular flippers, with blunt tips; broad and triangular flukes, with a concave trailing edge
- HEAD: long beak with a series of bristles; steep bulbous forehead
- COLOR: gray to white/pink above and light below; some individuals are totally pink

WHALE WATCHING

- WHEN TO GO: *August to November*
- WHERE TO GO: *Manaus, Brazil*
- SURFACE BEHAVIOUR: *seen alone or in small groups of two to three animals; moves slowly; surfaces at a shallow angle, showing melon, tip of rostrum, and dorsal ridge; performs high, arching rolls; sometimes curious; does not bow ride; aerial behavior is rare*

FAMILY KOGIIDAE

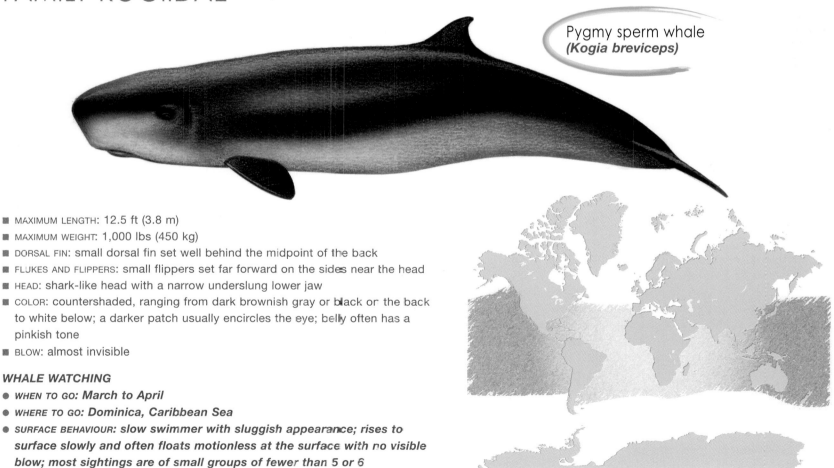

Pygmy sperm whale
(Kogia breviceps)

- MAXIMUM LENGTH: 12.5 ft (3.8 m)
- MAXIMUM WEIGHT: 1,000 lbs (450 kg)
- DORSAL FIN: small dorsal fin set well behind the midpoint of the back
- FLUKES AND FLIPPERS: small flippers set far forward on the sides near the head
- HEAD: shark-like head with a narrow underslung lower jaw
- COLOR: countershaded, ranging from dark brownish gray or black on the back to white below; a darker patch usually encircles the eye; belly often has a pinkish tone
- BLOW: almost invisible

WHALE WATCHING

- WHEN TO GO: *March to April*
- WHERE TO GO: *Dominica, Caribbean Sea*
- SURFACE BEHAVIOUR: *slow swimmer with sluggish appearance; rises to surface slowly and often floats motionless at the surface with no visible blow; most sightings are of small groups of fewer than 5 or 6 individuals; undemonstrative; does not show flukes on diving*

Dwarf sperm whale
(Kogia sima)

- ■ MAXIMUM LENGTH: 9 ft (2.7 m)
- ■ MAXIMUM WEIGHT: 600 lbs (272 kg)
- ■ DEPTH OF THE IMMERSION: to at least 980 ft (300 m)
- ■ DORSAL FIN: larger dorsal fin than the pygmy sperm whale, generally set near the middle of the back
- ■ FLUKES AND FLIPPERS: falcate, pointed dorsal fin
- ■ HEAD: shark-like head, but more pointed snout
- ■ COLOR: countershaded, with a brownish-gray to white coloration; ring of darker color surrounds each eye; belly often has a pinkish tinge
- ■ BLOW: invisible

WHALE WATCHING
- ● *WHEN TO GO: March to April*
- ● *WHERE TO GO: Dominica, Caribbean Sea*
- ● *SURFACE BEHAVIOUR: shy and undemonstrative when observed at sea, and difficult to detect; does not lift flukes when diving; aerial behavior rarely seen, although breaching sometimes occurs; slow swimmer; often floats motionless at the surface*

FAMILY MONODONTIDAE

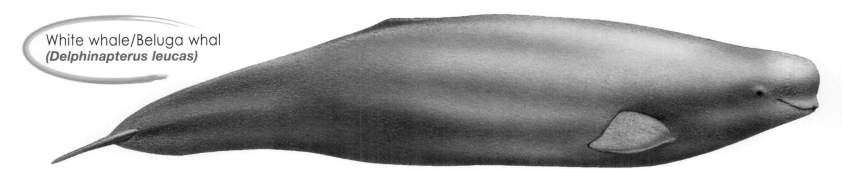

White whale/Beluga whal
(Delphinapterus leucas)

- ■ MAXIMUM LENGTH: 18 ft (5.5 m)
- ■ MAXIMUM WEIGHT: 3,500 (1,600 kg)
- ■ DURATION OF THE IMMERSION: up to 25 minutes
- ■ DEPTH OF THE IMMERSION: up to 3,300 ft (1,000 m)
- ■ DORSAL FIN: no dorsal fin
- ■ FLUKES AND FLIPPERS:short rounded flippers with sometimes curled tips in adult males; small flukes that often have a convex trailing edge
- ■ HEAD: small bulbous head with a very short beak; there is often a visible neck
- ■ COLOR: at birth, white whales are creamy pale gray, and they rapidly turn dark gray to brownish-gray. They whiten as they age, reaching pure white color between five and 12 years of age; some adults may have a yellowish tinge
- ■ BLOW: indistinct

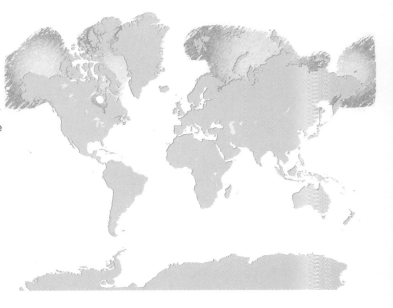

WHALE WATCHING
- ● *WHEN TO GO: June to September*
- ● *WHERE TO GO: only found in high latitudes of the Northern Hemisphere. Sites include lower St. Lawrence River, Quebec, Canada; Baffin Island, Nunavut, Canada; Churchill, Manitoba, Canada; Greenland*
- ● *SURFACE BEHAVIOUR: can be very active during the summer when they aggregate in large numbers in shallow estuaries; spyhopping, tail waving, fluke-slapping*

Narwhal
(Monodon monoceros)

- **MAXIMUM LENGTH**: 16 ft (4.8 m)
- **MAXIMUM WEIGHT**: 3,500 lbs (1,600 kg)
- **DURATION OF THE IMMERSION**: 7 to 20 minutes
- **DEPTH OF THE IMMERSION**: up to 3,800 ft (1,160 m)
- **DORSAL FIN**: no dorsal fin
- **FLUKES AND FLIPPERS**: short, blurt flippers that curl up at the tips in adults; flukes of adults are straight to concave on the leading edge, and convex on the trailing edge; they are deeply notched and the tips tend to curl upwards, especially in older animals
- **HEAD**: bulbous head with little or no beak; in males the left tooth grows out through the front of the head, starting at about two to three years of age and becomes a left-hand spiraled tusk up to 9 ft (2.7 m) long
- **COLOR**: young narwhals are uniformly gray to brownish-gray; as animals age, they darken to all black and then white mottling develops; at this stage, they appear spotted and belly becomes light gray to white, with some dark mottling; lightening continues with age, and older animals often appear nearly white, with some black mottling still remaining on top and front of the head, along dorsal ridge, flukes and flippers
- **BLOW**: indistinct

WHALE WATCHING

- **WHEN TO GO**: *June to September*
- **WHERE TO GO**: *found mostly above the Arctic Circle year-round. Sites include Greenland; Nunavut, Canada*
- **SURFACE BEHAVIOUR**: *shy and wary of boats; may float motionless at surface with part of back, tusk or flipper visible; occasionally lifts flukes upon diving*

FAMILY PHOCOENIDAE

Finless porpoise
(Neophocaena phocaenoides)

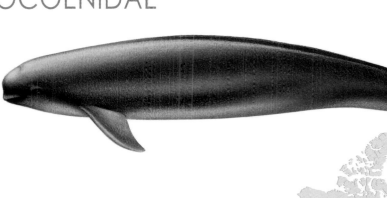

- **MAXIMUM LENGTH**: 7.5 ft (2.3 m)
- **MAXIMUM WEIGHT**: 154 lbs (70 kg)
- **DORSAL FIN**: no dorsal fin, but a long, shallow dorsal ridge
- **FLUKES AND FLIPPERS**: large flippers, with rounded tips; flukes have a concave trailing edge
- **HEAD**: rounded head, with no beak
- **COLOR**: predominantly gray

WHALE WATCHING

- **WHEN TO GO**: *year-round*
- **WHERE TO GO**: *Hong Kong*
- **SURFACE BEHAVIOUR**: *fast and agile swimmer, making high-speed sharp turns when chasing prey; does not bowride; can be shy of boats*

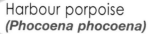

Harbour porpoise
(Phocoena phocoena)

- MAXIMUM LENGTH: 6 ft (1.8 m)
- MAXIMUM WEIGHT: 154 lbs (70 kg)
- DURATION OF THE IMMERSION: up to 5 minutes
- DEPTH OF THE IMMERSION: up to 725 ft (221 m)
- DORSAL FIN: short, wide-based, triangular dorsal fin, generally with small bumps on the leading edge
- FLUKES AND FLIPPERS: small flippers, rounded at the tips; flukes have a concave trailing edge, and are divided by a prominent median notch; rounded tips
- HEAD: blunt, short-beaked head
- COLOR: dark gray on the back and white on the belly

WHALE WATCHING

- *WHEN TO GO:* **May to September**
- *WHERE TO GO:* **Western Isles, Scotland; Vancouver Island, British Columbia, Canada**
- *SURFACE BEHAVIOUR:* **travels in small groups of fewer than five or six animals; never approaches boats to ride bow waves; often avoids vessels; back rolling quickly through the surface, sometimes splashing**

Dall's porpoise
(Phocoenoides dalli)

- MAXIMUM LENGTH: 8 ft (2.4 m)
- MAXIMUM WEIGHT: 440 lbs (200 kg)
- DORSAL FIN: wide-based triangular dorsal fin, with a falcate tip
- FLUKES AND FLIPPERS: small flippers placed near the head; flukes have straight or even slightly convex trailing edges with a notch in the middle
- HEAD: small head with a short beak, and no demarcation from the melon
- COLOR: strikingly marked, with a black body and bright white lateral patches; there is white to light gray "frosting" on the upper portion of the dorsal fin and the trailing edges of the flukes

WHALE WATCHING

- *WHEN TO GO:* **May to September**
- *WHERE TO GO:* **Vancouver Island, British Columbia, Canada**
- *SURFACE BEHAVIOUR:* **fastest swimmer of all small cetaceans; when swimming rapidly, slices along the surface, producing a characteristic V-shaped spray; avid bowrider; found in small groups of two to 12 animals**

FAMILY PHYSETERIDAE

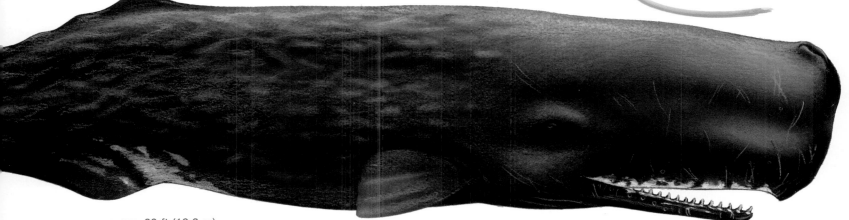

- ■ MAXIMUM LENGTH: 60 ft (18.3 m)
- ■ MAXIMUM WEIGHT: 125,000 lbs (57,000 kg)
- ■ DURATION OF THE IMMERSION: 30-45 minutes to more than an hour
- ■ DEPTH OF THE IMMERSION: most commonly about 1,300 ft (400 m) but up to 10,000 ft (3,200 m)
- ■ DORSAL FIN: thick, low, rounded dorsal hump and a series of bumps on the dorsal ridge of the tail stock
- ■ FLUKES AND FLIPPERS: short and wide flippers; broad and triangular flukes with a nearly straight trailing edge
- ■ HEAD: large head, one-quarter to one-third of the total body length. The lower jaw is much narrower than the upper jaw
- ■ COLOR: predominantly black to brownish-gray, with white areas around the mouth and often on the belly. White scratches and scars are common on the bodies, especially the heads, of some large adults
- ■ BLOW: bushy blow projects up to 16 ft (5 m), and is directed forward and to the left

WHALE WATCHING

- ● WHEN TO GO: *year-round (Kaikoura, Baja California, Dominica); May to September (Andenes); May to October (Azores)*
- ● WHERE TO GO: *cosmopolitan species. Sites include Baja California, Mexico; Kaikoura, New Zealand; Dominica, Caribbean Sea; Andenes, Norway; Azores*
- ● SURFACE BEHAVIOUR: *shows flukes prior to a deep dive, holding them high and perpendicular; most common aerial behaviors are breaching and fluke-slapping*

FAMILY ZIPHIIDAE

Arnoux's beaked whale and
Baird's beaked whale
(Berardius arnuxii/berardius bairdii)

- ■ BERARDIUS BAIRDII
- ■ BERARDIUS ARNUXII

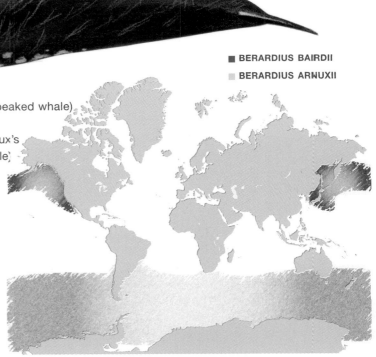

- ■ MAXIMUM LENGTH: 32 ft (9.8 m) (Arnoux's beaked whale) and 42 ft (12.8 m) (Baird's beaked whale)
- ■ MAXIMUM WEIGHT: 24,000 lbs (11,000 kg) (Baird's beaked whale)
- ■ DURATION OF THE IMMERSION: 15 to 25 minutes, but sometimes more than an hour (Arnoux's beaked whale); 11 to 30 minutes, sometimes more than an hour (Baird's beaked whale)
- ■ DEPTH OF THE IMMERSION: up to 3,300 ft (1,000 m) (Baird's beaked whale)
- ■ DORSAL FIN: small, triangular dorsal fin set far back on body
- ■ FLUKES AND FLIPPERS: short rounded flippers
- ■ HEAD: small head with a long tube-like beak
- ■ COLOR: gray body with many scars
- ■ BLOW: low and diffuse blow, often visible at a distance

WHALE WATCHING

- ● WHEN TO GO: *September to October*
- ● WHERE TO GO: *Monterey Bay, California, USA*
- ● SURFACE BEHAVIOUR: *shy of boats and difficult to approach, but can be active at the surface, breaching, spyhopping, fluke- and flipper-slapping*

Northern bottlenose whale and Southern bottlenose whale (*Hyperoodon ampullatus/planifrons*)

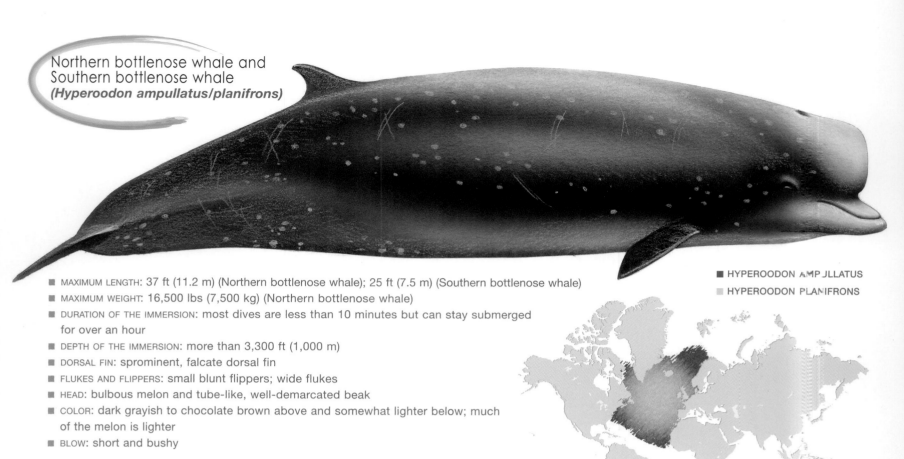

- MAXIMUM LENGTH: 37 ft (11.2 m) (Northern bottlenose whale); 25 ft (7.5 m) (Southern bottlenose whale)
- MAXIMUM WEIGHT: 16,500 lbs (7,500 kg) (Northern bottlenose whale)
- DURATION OF THE IMMERSION: most dives are less than 10 minutes but can stay submerged for over an hour
- DEPTH OF THE IMMERSION: more than 3,300 ft (1,000 m)
- DORSAL FIN: sprominent, falcate dorsal fin
- FLUKES AND FLIPPERS: small blunt flippers; wide flukes
- HEAD: bulbous melon and tube-like, well-demarcated beak
- COLOR: dark grayish to chocolate brown above and somewhat lighter below; much of the melon is lighter
- BLOW: short and bushy

WHALE WATCHING

- WHEN TO GO: *December to March (Antarctic Peninsula); May to September (Iceland)*
- WHERE TO GO: *Antarctic Peninsula (Southern bottlenose whale); Húsavík, Iceland (Northern bottlenose whale)*
- SURFACE BEHAVIOUR: *can be curious of vessels; breach and perform other aerial behaviors*

■ HYPEROODON AMPULLATUS
■ HYPEROODON PLANIFRONS

Blainville's beaked whale (*Mesoplodon densirostris*)

- MAXIMUM LENGTH: 15 ft (4.7 m)
- MAXIMUM WEIGHT: 2,300 lbs (1,033 kg)
- DURATION OF THE IMMERSION: up to an hour
- DEPTH OF THE IMMERSION: up to 4,600 ft (1,400 m)
- DORSAL FIN: small dorsal fin located about two-thirds of the way back from the snout tip
- FLUKES AND FLIPPERS: small and narrow flippers; un-notched flukes
- HEAD: small and narrow head; flattened forehead and moderately long beak; distinctive mouth line with abrupt arching about halfway along lower jaw; two teeth usually visible in middle of lower jaw in adult males
- COLOR: brownish or blue-gray above and lighter below; white scratches on body

WHALE WATCHING

- WHEN TO GO: *January to August*
- WHERE TO GO: *Bahamas, Caribbean Sea*
- SURFACE BEHAVIOUR: *often lifts beaks out of the water upon surfacing*

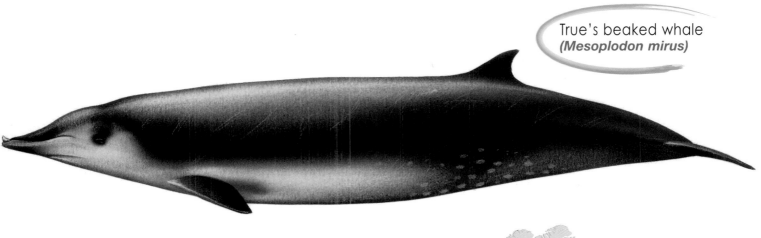

True's beaked whale
(Mesoplodon mirus)

- ■ MAXIMUM LENGTH: 18 ft (5.5 m)
- ■ MAXIMUM WEIGHT: 3,100 lbs (1,400 kg)
- ■ DORSAL FIN: small dorsal fin located about two-thirds of the way back from the snout tip
- ■ FLUKES AND FLIPPERS: small and narrow flippers; un-notched flukes
- ■ HEAD: rounded and prominent melon; medium-sized beak; dark ring around the eye
- ■ COLOR: dark blue or brownish gray above and slightly paler below
- ■ BLOW: low and indistinct

WHALE WATCHING
- ● *WHEN TO GO: March to July*
- ● *WHERE TO GO: Bay of Biscay, between France and Spain*
- ● *SURFACE BEHAVIOUR: occasionally breaches*

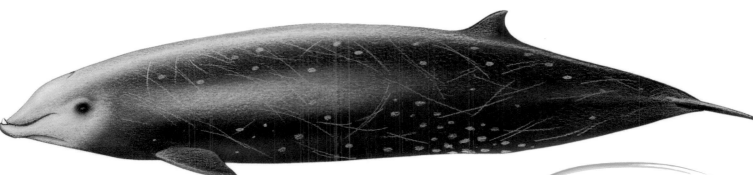

- ■ MAXIMUM LENGTH: 23 ft (7 m)
- ■ MAXIMUM WEIGHT: 6,600 ft (3,000 kg)
- ■ DURATION OF THE IMMERSION: up to 40 minutes
- ■ DEPTH OF THE IMMERSION: over 656 ft (200 m)
- ■ DORSAL FIN: small and falcate dorsal fin, set about two-thirds of the way back from the snout tip
- ■ FLUKES AND FLIPPERS: large flukes; small, rounded flippers that can be tucked into "flipper pockets"
- ■ HEAD: short beak; smoothly-sloping forehead; mouth line that is curved along most its length, with an upturn at the rear
- ■ COLOR: dark gray to light rusty brown body, with lighter areas around head and belly; adults are generally covered with scratches
- ■ BLOW: low and diffuse, often directed slightly forward

Cuvier's beaked whale
(Ziphius cavirostris)

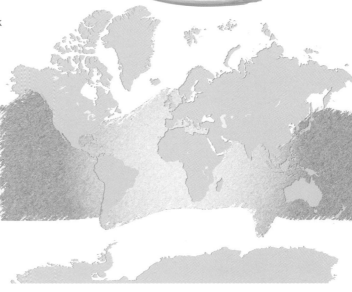

WHALE WATCHING
- ● *WHEN TO GO: March to May (Bay of Biscay); year-round (Hawaii); April to September (Ligurian Sea)*
- ● *WHERE TO GO: Bay of Biscay, Spain; Hawaii; Ligurian Sea, between France and Italy*
- ● *SURFACE BEHAVIOUR: can be difficult to approach; have been observed breaching occasionally*

BIBLIOGRAPHY

Bejder, Lars, et al. 2006. *Decline in relative abundance of bottlenose dolphins exposed to long-term disturbance.* Conservation Biology 20: 1791-1798.

Berman-Kowalewski, et al. 2010. *Association between blue whale (Balaenoptera musculus) mortality and ship strikes along the California coast.* Aquatic Mammals 36 (1): 59-66.

Berta, Annalisa, James Sumich, and Kit Kovacs. 2006. *Marine Mammals: Evolutionary Biology.* 2nd edition. Elsevier.

Bortolotti, Dan. 2009. *Wild Blue: A Natural History of the World's Largest Animal.* Toronto: Thomas Allen Publishers.

Byatt, Andrew, Alastair Fothergill, and Martha Holmes. 2001. *The Blue Planet: A Natural History of the Oceans.* New York: DK Publishing.

Cahill, Tim. 2000. *Dolphins.* Washington, D.C.: National Geographic Society.

Calambokidis, John, et al. 2009. *Insights into the population structure of blue whales in the Eastern North Pacific from recent sightings and photographic identification.* Marine Mammal Science. 25 (4): 816-832.

Carwardine, Mark. 2006. *Whales and Dolphins.* London: HarperCollins Publishers.

Chen, Lian, et al. 2010. *Microsatellite variation and significant population genetic structure of endangered finless porpoises (Neophocaena phocaenoides) in Chinese coastal waters and the Yangtze River.* Marine Biology. 157:1453-1462.

Connor, Richard C. 2007. *Dolphin social intelligence: complex alliance relationships in bottlenose dolphins and a consideration of selective environments for extreme brain size evolution in mammals.* Phil. Trans. R. Soc. B. 362: 587-602.

Cullon, Donna L., et al. 2009. *Persistent organic pollutants in Chinook salmon (Oncorhynchus tshawytscha): Implications for resident killer whales of British Columbia and adjacent waters.* Environmental Toxicology and Chemistry. 28 (1): 148-161.

Dalebout, M.L., et al. 2004. *A comprehensive and validated molecular taxonomy of beaked whales, Family Ziphiidae.* Journal of Heredity. 95 (6): 459-473.

Darling, James D., Meagan E. Jones, and Charles P. Nicklin. 2006. *Humpback whale songs: Do they organize males during the breeding season?* Behaviour. 143: 1051-1101.

Darling, James D., Charles Nicklin, Kenneth S. Norris, Hal Whitehead, and Bernd Würsig. 1995. *Whales, Dolphins and*

Porpoises. Washington, D.C.: National Geographic Society.

Day, Trevor. 2006. *Whale Watcher: A Global Guide to Watching Whales, Dolphins and Porpoises in the Wild.* New York: Firefly Books.

Dudzinksi, Kathleen M., and Toni Frohoff. 2008. *Dolphin Mysteries: Unlocking the Secrets of Communication.* New Haven: Yale University Press.

Dumont, Jean-Michel, and Rémy Marion. 1998. *On the Trail of Whales.* New York: Barron's Nature Travel Guides.

Fisheries and Oceans Canada. 2008. *Recovery Strategy for the Northern and Southern Killer Whales (Orcinus orca) in Canada.* Species at Risk Act Recovery Strategy Series, Fisheries & Oceans Canada, Ottawa.

Ford, John K. B., Graeme M. Ellis, Peter F. Olesiuk, and Kenneth C. Balcomb. 2009. *Linking killer whale survival and prey abundance: Food limitations in the oceans' apex predator?* Biology Letters. doi: 10.1098/rsbl.2009.0468.

Ford, John K. B, and Randall R. Reeves. 2008. *Fight or flight: antipredator strategies of baleen whales.* Mammal Review. 38: 50-86.

Ford, John K. B., and Graeme M. Ellis. 2006. *Selective foraging by fish-eating killer whales Orcinus orca in British Columbia.* Marine Ecology Progress Series. 316: 185-199.

Ford, John K.B., Graeme M. Ellis, and Kenneth C. Balcomb. 2000. *Killer Whales: The Natural History and Genealogy of Orcinus Orca in British Columbia and Washington.* Vancouver: University of British Columbia Press.

Ford, John K.B., and Graeme M. Ellis. 1999. *Transients: Mammal-Hunting Killer Whales.* Vancouver: UBC Press.

Forestell, Paul H., and Gregory D. Kaufman. 2008. *Humpbacks of Hawai'i: The Long Journey Back.* Hawai'i: Island Heritage Publishing.

Francis, Daniel, and Gil Hewlett. 2007. *Operation Orca: Springer, Luna and the Struggle to Save West Coast Killer Whales.* Madeira Park: Harbour Publishing.

Frère, Céline H., et al. 2010. *Home range overlap, matrilineal and biparental kinship drive female associations in bottlenose dolphins.* Animal Behaviour. 80: 481-486.

Frohoff, Toni, and Brenda Peterson, eds. 2003. *Between Species: Celebrating the Dolphin-Human Bond.* San Francisco: Sierra Club Books.

Gazda, Stefanie K., Richard C. Connor, and Robert K. Edgar. 2005. *A division of labour with role specialization in group-*

hunting bottlenose dolphins (Tursiops truncatus) off Cedar Key, Florida. 2005.Proceedings of the Royal Society B. 272: 135-140.

Gero, Shane, Dan Engelhaupt, Luke Rendell, and Hal Whitehead. 2009. *Who cares? Between-group variation in alloparental caregiving in sperm whales.* Behavioral Ecology. 20: 838-843.

Gibson, Quincy A., and Janet Mann. 2008. *The size, composition and function of wild bottlenose dolphin (Tursiops sp.) mother-calf groups in Shark Bay, Australia.* Animal Behaviour. 76: 389-405.

Gibson, Quincy A., and Janet Mann. 2008. *Early social development in wild bottlenose dolphins: sex differences, individual variation and maternal influence.* Animal Behaviour. 76: 375-387.

Hanson, Bradley M., et al. 2010. *Species and stock identification of prey consumed by endangered southern resident killer whales in their summer range.* Endangered Species Research. 11: 69-82.

Heynig, John E. 1995. *Masters of the Ocean Realm: Whales, Dolphins, Porpoises.* Vancouver: UBC Press.

Hoare, Philip. 2010. *The Whale: In Search of the Giants of the Sea.* New York: HarperCollins Publishers.

Holt, Marla. M., et al. 2009. *Speaking up: Killer whales (Orcinus orca) increase their call amplitude in response to vessel noise.* Journal of Acoustical Society of America. 125 (1): EL27-EL32.

Jefferson, Thomas A., Marc A. Webber, and Robert L. Pitman. 2008. *Marine Mammals of the World: A Comprehensive Guide to their Identification.* London: Elsevier.

Jones, David. 1998. *Whales.* Vancouver: Whitecap Books.

Kelsey, Elin. 2009. *Watching Giants: The Secret Lives of Whales.* Berkeley: University of California Press.

Knudtson, Peter 1996. *Orca: Visions of the Killer Whale.* Vancouver: Greystone Books.

Krützen, Michael, et al. 2005. *Cultural transmission of tool use in bottlenose dolphins.* PNAS 102: 8939-8943.

Laland, Kevin N., and Bennett G. Galef, eds. 2009. *The question of Animal Culture.* Cambridge: Harvard University Press.

Lusseau, David. 2007. *Evidence for social role in a dolphin social network.* Evolutionary Ecology. 21 (3): 357-366.

Lusseau, David. 2006. *Why do dolphins jump? Interpreting the behavioural repertoire of bottlenose dolphins (Tursiops sp.) in Doubtful Sound, New Zealand.* Behavioural Processes. 73: 257-265.

Mann, Janet, and Brooke L. Sargeant. 2009. *Developmental evidence for foraging traditions in wild bottlenose dolphins.* Animal Behaviour. 78: 715-721.

Mann, Janet, et al. 2008. *Why do Dolphins carry sponges?* PLoS ONE 3 (12): e3868. Doi:10.1371

Mann, Janet, Richard C. Connor, Peter L. Tyack, and Hal Whitehead, eds. 2000. *Cetacean Societies: Field Studies of Dolphins and Whales.* Chicago: University of Chicago Press.

Mason, Adrienne. 1999. *Whales, Dolphins, and Porpoises.* Vancouver: Altitude Publishing.

Marx, Felix G., and Mark D. Uhen. 2010. *Climate, critters, and cetaceans: Cenozoic drivers of the evolution of modern whales.* Science. 327: 993-996.

Matkin, Craig.O., et al. 2007. *Ecotypic variation and predatory behavior of killer whales in the Eastern Aleutian Islands, Alaska.* Fisheries Bulletin. 105: 74-87.

Morin, Phillip A., et al. 2010. *Complete mitochondrial genome phylogeographic analysis of killer whales (Orcinus orca) indicates multiple species.* Genome Research. 20 (7): 908-916.

Perrin, William, Bernd Würsig, and J. G. M. Thewissen, eds. 2008. *Encyclopedia of Marine Mammals, Second Edition.* San Diego: Academic Press.

Rayne, Sierra, et al. 2004. *PBDEs, PBBs, and PCNs in three communities of free-ranging killer whales (Orcinus orca) from the Northeastern Pacific Ocean.* Environmental Science and Technology. 38: 4293-4299.

Reeves, Randall R., Brian D. Smith, Enrique A. Crespo, and Guiseppe Notarbartolo di Sciara. 2003. *Dolphins, Whales and Porpoises: 2002-2010 Conservation Action Plan for the World's Cetaceans.* World Conservation Union.

Reeves, Randall R., Brent S. Stewart, Phillip J. Clapham, James A. Powell. 2008. *Guide to Marine Mammals of the World.* New York: Alfred A. Knopf.

Ross, Peter S. 2006. *Fireproof killer whales (Orcinus orca): Flame-retardant chemicals and the conservation imperative in the charismatic icon of British Columbia, Canada.* Canadian Journal of Fisheries and Aquatic Sciences. 63: 224-234.

Ross, Peter S., et al. 2000. *High PCB concentrations in free-ranging pacific killer whales, Orcinus orca: Effects of age, sex and dietary preference.* Marine Pollution Bulletin 40 (6): 504-515.

Schulz, Tyler, Hal Whitehead, Shane Gero, and Luke Rendell. 2010. *Individual vocal production in a sperm whale (Physeter*

macrocephalus) social unit. Marine mammal Science.

Schulz, Tyler M., Hal Whitehead, Shane Gero, and Luke Rendel. 2008. *Overlapping and matching of codas in vocal interactions between sperm whales: Insights into communication function.* Animal Behaviour. 76: 977-1988.

Shirihai, Hadoram, and Brett Jarrett. 2006. *Whales, Dolphins, and Other Marine Mammals of the World.* Princeton: Princeton University Press.

Slater, Graham J., et al. 2010. *Diversity versus disparity and the radiation of modern cetaceans.* Proceedings of the Royal Society B. 277: 3097-3104.

Spalding, David A.E. 1998. *Whales of the West Coast.* Madeira Park: Harbour Publishing.

Turvey, Samuel T., et al 2010. *Spatial and temporal extinction dynamics in a freshwater cetacean.* Proceedings of the Royal Society B. 277:3139-3147.

Ward. Eric J., et al. 2009. *The role of menopause and reproductive senescence in a long-lived social mammal.* Frontiers in Zoology. 6:4.

Whitehead, Hal. 2010 *Conserving and managing animals that learn socially and share cultures.* Learning and Behaviour. 38 (3): 329-336.

Whitehead, Hal, Amanda Coakes, Nathalie Jaquet, Susan Lusseau. 2008. *Movements of sperm whales in the tropical Pacific.* Marine Ecology Progress Series. 361: 291-300.

Whitehead, Hal, Luke Rendell, Richard W. Osborne, and Bernd Würsig. 2004. *Culture and conservation of non-humans with reference to whales and dolphins: review and new directions.* Biological Conservation. 120: 427-437.

Whitehead, Hal. 2003 *Sperm whales: Social Evolution in the Ocean.* Chicago: University of Chicago Press.

Wilson, Ben. 1998. *Dolphins of the World.* Stillwater: Voyageur Press.

Würtz, Maurizio, and Nadia Repetto. 2009. *Whales and Dolphins.* Vercelli: White Star Publishers.

Yurk, Harald, Lance G. Barrett-Lennard, John K. B. Ford, and Craig O. Matkin. 2002. *Cultural transmission within maternal lineages: Vocal clans in resident killer whales in Southern Alaska.* Animal behaviour. 63: 1103-1119.

Zhao, Xiujiang, et al. 2008 *Abundance and conservation status of the Yangtze finless porpoise in the Yangtze River, China.* Biological Conservation. 141:3006-3018.

INDEX

PHOTO CREDITS

Aaron S. Fink/Agefotostock: page 178 - Africa Wings/Agefotostock: page 225 - Alaska Stock Images/National Geographic Stock: pages 4-5 - Alexander Safonov/Getty Images: page 139 - Art Wolfe: page 204 - Bob Cranston/Seapics.com: pages 114-115 - Brandon Cole/Naturepl.com/Contrasto: page 230 - Brandon Cole/Photolibrary Group: pages 70-71 - Brandon Cole: pages 38-39, 122, 122-123, 124-125, 125, 126-127, 152, 188-189 - Centre for Dolphin/Agefotostock: pages 180-181 - Chijimatsu/e-Photography/Seapics.com: page 91 - Christopher Swann/Agefotostock: pages 190-191 - Corbis/Photolibrary Group: page 73 - Dave B. Fleetham/Photolibrary Group: pages 56-57, 58-59, 78-79 - David B. Fleetham/Seapics.com: pages 30, 162-163 - David B. Fleetham/Bluegreen Pictures: pages 174-175 - Doug Perrine /Photolibrary Group: pages 72-73 - Doug Perrine/Bluegreen Pictures: pages 119, 134-135 - Doug Perrine/Naturepl.com/Contrasto: pages 92-93, 231, 232-233 - Doug Perrine/Seapics.com: pages 34-35, 36, 62, 63, 94-95, 96-97, 118-119, 120-121, 126, 158-159, 214-215 - Drew Bradley/Seapics.com: pages 222-223 - Duncan Murrell/Agefotostock: pages 108-109, 110-111 - Eric Cheng/Getty Images: pages 206-207 - Flip Nicklin/Getty Images: pages 194-195 - Flip Nicklin/Minden/National Geographic Stock: pages 203, 216, 218 - Franco Banfi/Agefotostock: pages 54, 54-55 - Franco Banfi/Photolibrary Group: pages 14-15 - Francois Gohier/Ardea: pages 117, 130-131 - Frank Wirth/Agefotostock: pages 132-133 - G. Lacz/Panda Photo: page 166 - Gerard Soury/Osf/Photolibrary Group: pages 196-197, 216-217 - Guenter Lenz/Photolibrary Group: page 92 - Gulf of Maine Prod/Agefotostock: pages 104-105, 105, 106 - H. Schmidbauer/Agefotostock: pages 82, 88-89 - Howard Hall/Photolibrary Group: pages 42-43 - Inoo /e-Photography/Seapics.com: pages 140-141 - James D. Watt/Seapics.com: pages 26, 146-147 - Janet Baxter/Agefotostock: pages 2-3 - Jason Heller/Getty Images: pages 136-137, 138-139 - Jeff Rotman: pages 176-177, 177, 228-229, 229 - John Hyde/Photolibrary Group: pages 64-65 - Jonathan Bird/Photolibrary Group: page 57 - Juniors Bildarchiv/Photolibrary Group: pages 68-69, 71, 166-167 - Juniors Bildarchiv/Tips: page 68 - Jurgen Freund/Bluegreen Pictures: pages 37 - Kelvin Aitken/Photolibrary Group: pages 48-49 - Kevin Schafer/Seapics.com: pages 86-87 - Kike Calvo/V & W/Seapics.com: page 40 - Lothar Lenz/Agefotostock: pages 46-47 - Luis Quinta/Seapics.com: pages 156-157 - Marc Chamberlain/Seapics.com: pages 160-161 - Mark Carwardine/Bluegreen Pictures: pages 44-45 - Mark Carwardine/Photolibrary Group: pages 41, 234-235 - Masa Ushioda /Seapics.com: pages 32-33, 152-153, 220, 221, 222 - Masa Ushioda/WaterF/Agefotostock: pages 7, 31 - Masa Ushioda/WaterF/Photolibrary Group: pages 172-173 - Michael S. Nolan/Agefotostock: pages 26-27, 28, 116, 154-155 - Michael S. Nolan/Seapics.com: pages 90, 112-113 - Norbert Probst/Photolibrary Group: pages 60-61 - Norbert Rosing/Getty Images: pages 204-205 - Paul A. Souders/Corbis: pages 192-193 - Paul Nicklen/National Geographic Stock: pages 50-51, 74-75, 76-77, 80-81, 202-203 - Phillip Colla/WWW.Oceanlight.com: pages 226-227 - Reinhard Dirscherl/Agefotostock: page 179 - Renee DeMartin/Corbis: page 18-19 - Richard Herrmann/Seapics.com: page 42 - Rob Lott/Getty Images: pages 128-129 - Robert L. Pitman/Seapics.com: pages 164-165 - Rodger Klein/Seapics.com: page 10 - Rolf Hicker/Photolibrary Group: pages 66-67 - Scott Hanson/Seapics.com: pages 12-13 - Shedd/Brenna Hernandez/Seapics.com: pages 168-169, 170-171, 171 - Splashdown Direct/Photolibrary Group: pages 187, 224 - Steven Kazlowski/Corbis: pages 200-201 - Sue Flood/Naturepl.com/Contrasto: pages 82-83, 84-85 - Sue Flood/Tartan Dragon/Osf/Photolibrary Group: page 151 - Thomas Kitchin & Victoria Hurst/Photolibrary Group: pages 16-17 - Tom & Pat Leeson/Ardea: pages 198-199 - Tui de Roy/Getty Images: page 186 - Wild Wonders of Europe/Lundgren/Bluegreen Pictures: page 219 - Wolfgang Poelzer/Agefotostock: page 53 - Wolfgang Poelzer/Photolibrary Group: page 52 - Wyland/Seapics.com: page 150 - Yva Momatiuk & John Eastcott/National Geographic Stock: page 107 - Yves Lefèvre/Biosphoto/Tips: pages 28-29, 148-149 - Drawings by Maurizio Würtz and Nadia Repetto/Archivio White Star: pages 240-269

WHITE STAR PUBLISHERS

WS White Star Publishers® is a registered trademark
property of Edizioni White Star s.r.l.

© 2011 Edizioni White Star s.r.l.
Via Candido Sassone, 24
13100 Vercelli, Italy
www.whitestar.it

978-88-544-0581-3
1 2 3 4 5 6   15 14 13 12 11

Printes in China